CITIES UNDER THE GUN

CITIES UNDER THE GUN

Images of Occupied Nashville and Chattanooga

BY James A. Hoobler

PHOTOGRAPHS BY George N. Barnard AND OTHERS

RUTLEDGE HILL PRESS

Nashville, Tennessee

Published in Nashville, Tennessee, by Rutledge Hill Press, Inc., 211 Seventh Avenue North, Nashville, Tennessee 37219.

Library of Congress Cataloging-in-Publication Data

Hoobler, James A.
    Cities under the gun.

    Includes index.
    1. Chattanooga, Battle of, 1863—Pictorial works. 2. Nashville, Battle of, 1864—Pictorial works. 3. Nashville (Tenn.)—Description—Views. 4. Chattanooga (Tenn.)—Description—Views. I. Barnard, George N. II. Title
E475.97.H66 1986   973.7'359   86-12702
ISBN 1-55853-355-9

DESIGNED BY Harriette Bateman
TYPOGRAPHY by ProtoType Graphics

2 3 4 5 6 7 8 — 99 98 97 96 95

I dedicate this volume
to two of my ancestors
who have given me
both my name and my interest in this subject.

JAMES WALKER

BATTERY A, 1ST OHIO LIGHT ARTILLERY

AND

ALLEN FIRESTONE

EARLY AMATEUR PHOTOGRAPHER

TABLE OF CONTENTS

FOREWORD 9

ACKNOWLEDGEMENTS 10

INTRODUCTION 11

NASHVILLE 15

THE ATHENS OF THE SOUTH 17

A MAGNIFICENT CAPITOL 29

RAILROADS IN NASHVILLE 41

UP ON COLLEGE HILL 55

A CITY OF BEAUTIFUL ARCHITECTURE 71

DOWNTOWN NASHVILLE 81

CHATTANOOGA 113

THE CITY AT MOCCASIN BEND 115

CHATTANOOGA BESIEGED 127

HOMES IN EARLY CHATTANOOGA 153

CHATTANOOGA AS A STAGING GROUND FOR INVASION 161

SHIPS, SAWMILLS, A BRIDGE, AND BOREDOM 191

RAILROAD TRESTLES 207

THE MAIN LINE OF SUPPLY 209

INDEX 222

FOREWORD

In the late summer of 1982, while I was vacationing in Washington, D.C., I decided to spend some time in the National Archives and the Library of Congress familiarizing myself with their photographs relating to Tennessee. As the War Between the States is an interest of mine and as I already knew that several photographs of the state made during the war were there, I decided to begin with that period. I was amazed to find hundreds of photographs of Nashville and Chattanooga on file. The cartographic and architectural division in Alexandria had drawings from Nashville and Chattanooga which also numbered in the hundreds. Making notes on all of this, I returned to Nashville.

I contacted the Tennessee State Library and Archives, the Tennessee State Museum, the Tennessee Historical Commission, the Metro Historical Commission, Historic Nashville, the Metro Nashville/Davidson County Public Library, the Chattanooga Area Historical Society, and the Chattanooga Public Library to see if any of these organizations knew of the existence of these materials. They did not. Because these pictures and drawings all related to Tennessee, I decided that the materials should be copied and "brought home."

I turned to friends and the membership of the Tennessee Historical Society and raised the money (largely through Kermit C. Stengel's generous gifts) to copy the collections and bring the copies to Tennessee from the National Archives and the Library of Congress. Kay Beasley and Bill Lafevor agreed to make slides of a number of the photographs and drawings so that I could give presentations on the collections. To date I have spoken to several thousand people on the material.

I have returned to Washington on vacation three other times to search further for materials and have been able to locate more on each trip. I know that more photographs exist at the United States Army Military History Institute at Carlisle Barracks, the Chicago Historical Society, the Western Reserve Historical Society, and the National Archives, but the amount of material already collected calls for the publication of the materials now at hand.

These photographs and drawings are a key that can unlock the past, graphically portraying conditions in the two occupied towns. They teach us much about warfare, urban life, architecture, engineering, the railroads, photography, and shipping on the rivers of the interior. I hope you find these images as fascinating as I do, for through them you can imagine life in these occupied towns.

ACKNOWLEDGEMENTS

Numerous individuals have assisted me in locating, copying, and identifying these photographs and architectural drawings. This book has taken several years to reach print, and I could not have completed it without their support and encouragement. Barbara Burger of the Still Picture Branch of the National Archives was particularly helpful in processing my orders for prints. John A. Dwyer, of the Cartographic/Architectural Branch of the National Archives, was similarly helpful with the drawings. Kermit C. Stengel largely paid for the copying done on the original prints in various respositories and has been very supportive of the whole undertaking.

Kay Beasley and Bill Lafevor made slides of many of the prints so that I could give lectures on the project as it progressed over the years. Ken Dubke of the National Park Service in Chattanooga has also supported this part of the work. Clara Swann of the Chattanooga Public Library was extremely helpful in identifying locations in Chattanooga. Dr. James Livingood, the distinguished Hamilton County historian, kindly agreed to meet with me to discuss the project. He is the preeminent authority on the history of Chattanooga, and our conversation was most helpful.

Other people who helped me to identify various aspects of these photographs include: Martha Carver, Steve Brown, Walter Durham, Paul Clements, Herb Peck, Ernest K. Johns, David Wright, Robert and Sue Ragland, Hume Parks, Shain Dennison, Fran Schell, Marylin Hughes, Ruth Jarvis, Bob Bell, and Richard Weesner.

Larry Stone, Mary Wheeler, and Genon Neblett at Rutledge Hill Press have been both encouraging and supportive. I have very much enjoyed working with them all. Harriette and Jim Batemen were the lay-out team, and they were a pleasure to work with. I am grateful to all of these people for the help they have given me.

James A. Hooper

May, 1986

INTRODUCTION

The state of Tennessee was greatly divided by the War Between the States and its political prelude. The western third of the state, which was strongly proslavery, pro-Democrat, and pro-Confederacy, was an integral part of the "Cotton Kingdom." The eastern third, which was primarily nonslave-owning, pro-Republican, and pro-Union, was politically the odd-man-out of Dixie— then and now. The middle third, a somewhat divided region, was basically proslavery, pro-Confederacy, and largely Democratic.

Tennessee's first vote to secede, on 9 February 1861, had been narrowly defeated by 59,449 for, and 68,282 against. However, on 6 May 1861 the legislature voted to call for a second referendum on secession since Fort Sumter had been attacked in April, which started the War Between the States. On 7 May 1861, Governor Isham G. Harris told the Tennessee legislature that he had agreed to a military league with the Confederacy. The legislature voted its approval, and on 8 June 1861 Tennesseans took the fateful step by voting 104,913 to 47,238 to leave the Union.

The overwhelming majority of those opposed to leaving the United States and joining the Confederate States of America were East Tennesseans. They held several meetings to discuss seceding from Tennessee and re-entering the Union. However, there was no clear pattern of opinion. Knoxville had voted 777 to 377 for secession. Hamilton County had voted 1,260 against secession and 854 for it, but Chattanooga, Hamilton's largest town, favored secession.

Since the Confederacy needed the rail lines running through East Tennessee to link Virginia to the deep South, Jefferson Davis decided to send a Confederate Army to hold East Tennessee in the Confederacy, even against the people's will. He selected a Whig political leader from Nashville, Felix Zollicoffer, to lead the Confederate forces because Zollicoffer was known and respected in East Tennessee. It was hoped that he could persuade the people to join with their southern neighbors in the Confederate cause. Guerilla activity flourished in East Tennessee—on both sides. The people did not change their minds, and Zollicoffer was killed in fighting near Cumberland Gap in January, 1862.

Meanwhile Nashville, where the vote had been overwhelmingly for secession, lay exposed and vulnerable, and in March, 1862, Federal troops moved into the town after the double Confederate humiliations at Fort Henry and Fort Donelson. Both forts had been taken and most of their defending troops were now prisoners of war. How ironic it was that Confederate-sympathizing Nashville was in Federal hands while pro-Unionist East Tennessee was held by the Confederates. Both now endured an experience known only in the South in the United States—military defeat, occupation, and humiliation at enemy hands. This searing emotional, economic, and psychological trauma has had repercussions down to today. More than anything else, this has made the South separate, different, unique.

During the summer of 1863, the Confederacy was dealt a double blow from which it would not recover. On the fourth of July, 1863,

Vicksburg, Mississippi, fell to General Grant, thus opening up all of the Mississippi River to Federal gun boats and dividing the Confederate States in two. The day before General Lee was defeated at Gettysburg, Pennsylvania, and the final Confederate offensive into the northern states was turned back.

Autumn of 1863 saw the Confederates defeat the Federals in North Georgia, at a place called Chickamauga, only to be defeated by Grant again at Chattanooga. Knoxville was liberated by Federal troops in September. This helped to bring about Bragg's Confederate defeat at Chattanooga because when Knoxville fell, the East Tennessee rail lines, so vital to the supplying of the Confederates in the deep South, were cut.

In March, 1864, with Southern hopes fading, General William T. Sherman was named commander of the Military Division of the Mississippi headquartered in Nashville. Assigned to him as official photographer was George N. Barnard. On 25 March when Sherman went on an inspection tour of his new command, visiting Pulaski, Huntsville, Stevenson, Bridgeport, Chattanooga, Knoxville, and Loudon, Barnard apparently accompanied him, for there are photographs by Barnard of Chattanooga, Knoxville, and Loudon.

Upon returning to Nashville, Barnard made nearly one hundred photographs of buildings either seized or built by and for the Federal Army of Occupation. He also made a photographic record of the military railroad trestles on the lines leading out of Nashville. About this same time, Captain J. F. Isom of the Post Quartermaster's office also began to document a number of the structures seized or constructed by the army in Nashville. He made several hundred detailed architectural drawings of them. Although the purpose for this documentation is not known, perhaps it was to be used to aid Captain William Driver's Board of Commissioners in settling war claims.

On 28 April 1864 Sherman moved his headquarters to Chattanooga to build an army of 100,000 men to invade the rebellious state of Georgia. Barnard continued to photograph both old and new structures, and army engineers continued to make detailed renderings of buildings that they created in Chattanooga.

On 5 May 1864, Sherman rode to Ringgold, Georgia, and launched his march to the sea. George Barnard accompanied him on this entire campaign, and it is primarily for the photographic documentation he did at that time that Barnard is remembered. His ominous views of a doomed Atlanta became widely known.

General William T. Sherman

It is unfortunate that George N. Barnard has been largely overlooked as an American pioneer in photography. Born in New York state in 1819, he was already experimenting with photography by 1832, only three years after its invention by Louis Daguerre in France. Barnard began his career in Oswego, New York, making the earliest known American spot news photographs there in 1847.

In 1854 Barnard moved to Syracuse, New York, where he began to make ambrotypes and melainotypes. During the 1850s he became increasingly respected and honored by his colleagues. In 1853 he was elected to serve as secretary of the New York State Daguerrean Association. In 1857 he was awarded the American Institute's bronze medal for inventing a process whereby photographs could be made upon wood, allowing wood engravings to be made directly from a photographic image.

The Kean Archives

George N. Barnard

room. This Rucker ambulance appears in several of his Nashville views. In Georgia he double printed his photographs to add dark ominous clouds, creating an image of doom and poignant foreboding.

In the 1870s Barnard worked in Chicago, where, during the Great Fire, he saved his best camera and lenses by holding them over his head in the Chicago River as he watched his studio—and the city—burn around him. Later he worked briefly in Painesville, Ohio, and in South Carolina, before returning to New York, where he helped George Eastman start a photographic business. Barnard and Eastman were both elected to membership in the Rochester Photographic Association on the same occasion in 1884.

Barnard lived the last eighteen years of his life in Oswego County, New York. He died there, all but forgotten, at Onondaga, on 4 February 1902.

In 1866 Barnard issued a book, *Photographic Views of Sherman's Campaign,* which contained sixty-one photographic prints of Nashville, Chattanooga, and the campaigns in Georgia and the Carolinas. At the time of its release, a review in *Harper's Weekly* said:

> These photographs are views of important places, of noted battle-fields, of military works; and, for the care and judgment in selecting the points of view, for the delicacy of execution, for scope of treatment, and for fidelity of representation, they surpass any other photographic views which have been produced in this country—whether relating to the war or otherwise. . . . Before seeing this collection of Mr. Barnard we could not have believed that there were such magnificent possibilities in an art so purely mechanical as to its mode of operation. Even the tints and cloud-scenery of the sky are exquisite in their perfection.

Photographic Views of Sherman's Campaign is Barnard's chief monument. *Cities Under the Gun: Images of Occupied Nashville and Chattanooga* is an attempt to build upon that. Much more is needed. Volumes on Georgia, South Carolina, and North Carolina should be done as well. With the publication of this book, I hope Barnard's reputation will be somewhat revived.

This book also contains some photographs of Nashville made by T. M. Schleier, who came to Nashville during the occupation and made an unknown number of photographs of the city, and by "Bailey of Nashville." These additions were recently discovered by Herb Peck. There are also photographs by unknown photographers.

In February, 1861, Barnard joined Mathew Brady's photographic crew in Washington, D.C., where he helped to photograph Lincoln's first inauguration and began to make some of the earliest *carte de visites* of our national leaders.

Barnard is one of only a few photographers mentioned in the official records of the Union Army. As an officially sanctioned photographer attached to Sherman's command, he was issued two pack mules, an armed escort, a driver, and a covered wagon to serve as a field dark

NASHVILLE

1 8 6 4

THE ATHENS OF THE SOUTH

Nashville sits upon a bluff overlooking the Cumberland River. Away from the river, it is in a beautiful natural bowl surrounded by a chain of hills. At the time it was settled, in 1779, it was far removed from other centers of European peoples, the nearest settlement being about 300 miles away, and was, as Theodore Roosevelt described it, "a great leap westward."

Situated on a navigable river midway between the Great Lakes and the Gulf Coast, and with the Natchez Trace and the Cumberland and Mississippi rivers giving it access to both regions, Nashville developed as a shipping and marketing center. The coming of rail and telegraph lines made it an important part of a national distribution and communication network. By 1860, only New Orleans could rival Nashville in size and importance south of the Ohio River in the West. In that year Nashville had a population of about 17,000, with another 13,000 in its suburbs. Its Public Square and Market Street were lined with wholesale and retail merchants and warehouses, and its wharf was constantly busy.

At the outbreak of the War Between the States, greater Nashville had a largely white population (about 24,000), with about 1,000 free blacks and 5,000 slaves. It was mainly Protestant, with twenty white congregations and four black ones. There were also two Roman Catholic churches and two Jewish synagogues. The Protestants jointly ran an orphanage. The Methodists and Baptists published religious materials, which they distributed to their denominations regionally.

Nashville also had developed as an educational center prior to the war. The medical department of the University of Nashville and the Shelby Medical College attracted a large number of students, making Nashville second only to Philadelphia as a medical center. A number of academies for young women, most notably the Nashville Female Academy and the St. Cecilia Academy, attracted students from near and far. The reputations of its educational institutions and their faculties earned the city the sobriquet, "the Athens of the South."

In 1843 Nashville became the permanent capital of Tennessee, and work began in 1845 on a capitol building. A penitentiary had been built west of town in 1830 and a state hospital for the insane south of town in 1833. The latter eventually became the city hospital, as in 1851 a larger hospital for the insane was built on Murfreesboro Turnpike southeast of Nashville.

Although the town lacked paved streets, it did have a municipal water system and a gaslight company. It also enjoyed two large theatres, the Adelphi, which had the second largest stage in America, and the New Theatre. Together these two houses brought in a variety of good theatrical productions to Nashville.

Large agricultural areas surrounded the city, with corn and tobacco being the chief crops. Belle Meade, a 5,300-acre farm to the southwest of town, was becoming the nation's premier Thoroughbred stud farm, while Belmont, a countryside summer retreat for the Acklen family, included a private zoo, a 300-foot-long conservatory for rare plants, the largest private art gallery in the South, and a bowling alley. Other large farms and estates circled Nashville and dotted the rich lands of nearby Sumner, Williamson, Robertson, Montgomery, Maury, and Rutherford counties.

Although Tennessee was the last state to leave the Union, when it did secede it was proposed in Nashville that the city would be chosen as the capital of the Confederacy. However, Tennessee lost out, first to Alabama and then to Virginia, and before long Tennessee even lost Nashville itself, for in March, 1862, it was captured by the Federal army, the first Confederate state capital to fall.

Nashville's defenses were nearly non-existent. The South had hoped that Kentucky would join the cause and that the Ohio River could thus be a defensible boundary. However, Kentucky remained neutral, and when the Confederacy invaded it, the Union counterinvaded and held it in the Union. The Confederates then pulled back to a weakly manned, ragged line of defense running from Fort Harris at Memphis through Fort Wright and Fort Pillow upstream on the Mississippi River, to Island Number Ten and Columbus, Kentucky. The defense line then jumped to the narrow neck of land separating the Tennessee and Cumberland rivers where Fort Henry and Fort Donelson were built. Fort Defiance guarded Clarksville downstream (north) from Nashville on the Cumberland. A handful of Confederate troops awaited a Federal invasion in Bowling Green, Kentucky, but the defensive line then disappeared until it reached the Cumberland Gap far to the east. The debacle caused by this poorly conceived and lightly manned defensive line was swift in coming.

On 19 January 1862, General Felix Zollicoffer, a Whig newspaper editor prior to the war and a Nashville resident, ordered his men into action at Mill Springs, or Fishing Creek, Kentucky, near Cumberland Gap. The whole engagement was tragicomic. Heavy fog and rain blanketed the mountainous area when the battle began. Wearing a bright yellow raincoat, the nearsighted General Zollicoffer took off his wet glasses and rode up to some nearby troops to speak to them. Unfortunately he approached the wrong army, and the Federal soldiers shot and killed him. This caused panic among the Confederate troops who hastily retreated.

A few weeks later, on 4 February, Federal gunboats plowed up the flood-swollen Tennessee River to Fort Henry. However, because the Confederate engineers had built Fort Henry within the floodplain, the flooding river overran the lower part of the fort before the Federal army did. Therefore General Lloyd Tilghman ordered his Confederate troops to evacuate across the peninsula to Fort Donelson while he remained behind with fifty-six artillerists to cover the evacuation; he then surrendered on 6 February. When news of this defeat reached General William Hardee, he pulled his troops out of Bowling Green and fled to Nashville.

Then all 17,000 of General Ulysses S. Grant's Federal troops, seven gunboats, and a few transports moved against the Confederates at Fort Donelson. Grant's foot soldiers marched across the peninsula and assaulted the fort from the landward side. Flag Officer Andrew Foote, who had taken his ships back down the Tennessee River, moved them into place on the Cumberland River to use the fire power of their big guns against the fort in conjunction with Grant's land based attack.

The Confederates had reinforced Fort Donelson with troops under generals John Floyd, Gideon Pillow, and Simon Buckner, bringing the garrison strength up to 15,000 men. Federal gunboats tested the strength of the fortification by shelling it on the twelfth and thirteenth. Fighting took place in earnest on 14 and 15 February, with the Confederates actually breaking out of the fort and reaching the Nashville road. That success made it possible for them to have escaped the invading army, but General Gideon Pillow panicked and fled back into the fort. The troops followed, and all was lost. The next day Grant demanded unconditional surrender. The fort and all of its defenders were delivered to him except the brilliant cavalry commander Nathan Bedford Forrest, who led his troops across a swollen creek to freedom. The Union had won a smashing victory. It had driven two wedges into the upper South, and had demoralized its foes.

When news arrived in Clarksville that Fort Defiance would be next, the name of the fort became a sad joke, as the soldiers dumped their cannons into the Cumberland River and fled. Nashville lay open, unprotected, vulnerable.

"The Great Panic" began on Sunday morning, 16 February 1862, when news finally reached Nashville of the capture of Fort Donelson and its defenders. Church services were disrupted throughout town. Mrs. Louisa Brown Pearl, wife of Nashville's first school superintendent, was one who stayed home that day. Her family had been divided. Earlier her husband had gone north to Detroit with their two daughters to remain there for the duration of the war. John, their son, had enlisted in C Company, First (Feild's) Tennessee Infantry, a Confederate troop. Louisa remained in Nashville to attempt to save their property and to maintain contact with John. Her diary reveals a fascinating glimpse of life in those terrifying times.

Feb. 16 Today has been a memorable day to Nashville. While Mr. F. [Foster, a boarder] was talking, a messenger came in and said that all was lost. The Federals would be here by four in the evening and telling us that Gov. [Isham G.] Harris had fled with the State papers and we must all look out for ourselves. Of course we were in great trepidation expecting the town would be shelled. The congregations assembling for worship were dismissed and people were seen hurrying to and fro like crazy people not knowing what to do. [General Albert Sidney] Johnston's army which lately evacuated Bowling Green commenced moving thru the city. We are informed that Nashville will make no resistance and we again hope that we may not be disturbed but everybody is on the move, hacks, carriages and drays are in requisition and by twelve nothing of the kind can be had for love or money—thousands have left town and are still going, leaving their houses empty. It is supposed that Fort Donaldson [sic] has fallen. Later we learn that it is not so, but that a terrible battle is still raging, so that blood flows in the trenches. Conflicting reports make me undecided what to do. I will stay where I am, if the army make no resistance. . . . I have picked up my clothing and some valuables where I can easily pack them and sit trembling by awaiting the great news. The gentlemen go out often to get the last report. The officers boarding with me encouraged us at dinner and said they would only fire at the gunboats to cover the retreat of Johnston's army. It is a sad, sad sight that army—four abreast they have been marching thro' the town all day in a solid column and will be till tomorrow noon. We fear fires tonight. May God preserve us.

During the next few days, military targets like the suspension bridge, the powder magazine, and certain riverboats were burned by the Confederates. Rioting broke out and some private property and Confederate warehouses were also looted. A rise in the river flooded areas of north Nashville. On 22 February, Louisa wrote, "Poor Nashville seems doomed." One day later, the Federal army reached Edgefield, a town immediately across the Cumberland River. There it remained until reinforced, and on 25 February the troops crossed the river in force, General Don Carlos Buell having arrived from Louisville via Bowling Green with 50,000 men. The military population of the city outnumbered the civilians by a ratio of one and one half to one.

' Rapid expansion of rail facilities and accommodations for the troops was essential under these circumstances. Once Federal troops had reached Nashville, they began to convert it into a war materiel storage depot for the entire war zone between the mountains and the Mississippi. It became a strategic forward staging area for the conquest of the interior South. Warehouses were seized and adapted to hold war goods; troops were garrisoned about the town to protect it from insurrection or invasion; homes, lands, and commercial buildings were taken over to house the occupying forces. Whole tent complexes were created north, west, south, and east of town. Hospitals were set up to care for the wounded from battles in the region and for those suffering from endemic diseases such as malaria, typhoid, cholera, yellow fever, and smallpox. Churches, schools, warehouses, homes, factories, stores, and even the capitol itself were pressed into service as military hospitals. Even this was not enough, and so tent hospitals were also erected. The entire purpose of life changed in occupied Nashville. All principal activities of the city were inexorably tied to the prosecution of the war, to the conquest of the Confederacy. Nashville had to be held at all costs.

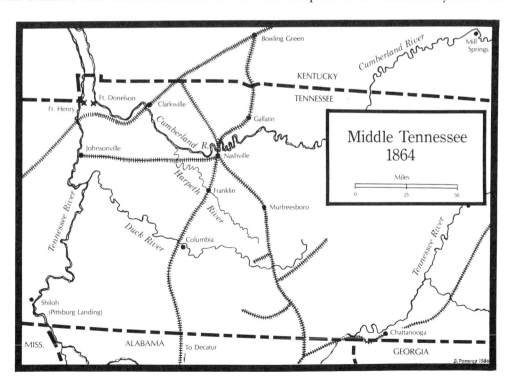

1. *Federal troops first reached Nashville on 25 February 1862, following the Confederate defeat at Fort Henry and Fort Donelson. When the population heard that Nashville had been left defenseless, a Great Panic ensued in which looting, rioting, arson, and flight occurred. It was precipitated by false rumors that the Federal gun boats and troops approaching the town would shell it and then burn it to the ground as an object lesson against sedition. No such plan had been formulated in Washington, however.*

On 4 March 1862 the first Federal army dress parade was held on Nashville's Public Square. Here the troops are lined along College Street on the west side of the Public Square. (OHIO HISTORICAL SOCIETY)

2. *Officers of the Quartermaster's department gather for a group photograph in July, 1864. It was their responsibility to feed, house, and clothe the Federal troops stationed in Nashville as well as to supply the troops in the field.* (TENNESSEE HISTORICAL SOCIETY)

3. *In this view of Nashville from the west, the state capitol is seen on the horizon to the extreme left and the state penitentiary, shown again in photograph 5, is just to its right nearer the photographer. The dirt road on the left is Spring Street, and as it leads into the town the towers of old First Presbyterian Church are seen above the third row of large tents. The Masonic Hall is across the street from the church.*

The tents in the foreground are a Federal army field hospital on Williams Street between Spring and Broad streets. The entrance to the hospital is shown in photograph 4.

Just to the right of the center, two houses are visible on the horizon. The one behind the tree to the left was the Robert Houston house and the one on the right was the Kirkpatrick house. These were near the corner of Mulberry Street and Broad Street. (NATIONAL ARCHIVES)

4. *The Cumberland Field Hospital was situated between Spring and Broad streets. A 384-tent complex with 2,304 beds, it covered 30 acres. The tents were floored and framed and had 6 beds each. Twenty-one frame buildings served the hospital. The ground plot shows its layout.* (NATIONAL ARCHIVES)

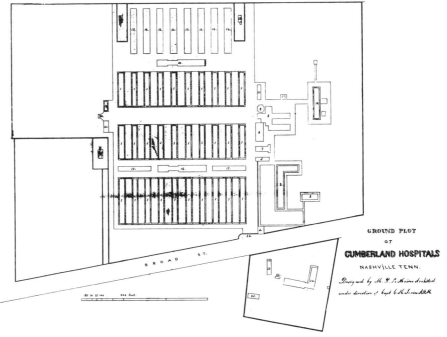

5. *David Morrison was the architect for the Tennessee State Penitentiary, built between 1828 and 1830 between Spring Street and Cedar Street, near present day Fifteenth Avenue. The Federal authorities incarcerated* *Confederates in the penitentiary during the occupation, which is the reason why it was fortified.* (T. M. SCHLEIER PHOTOGRAPH FROM THE COLLECTION OF HERB PECK)

[7]

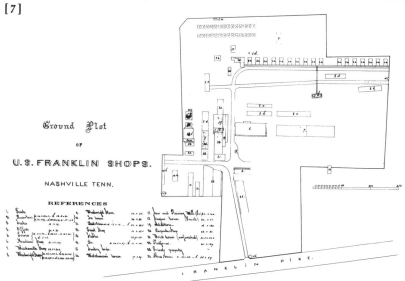

6-7. *The United States Franklin Shops were on the Franklin Turnpike south of Nashville. In photograph 6, the building on the left was a saw and planing mill, carpenter's shop, and engine house. The building with the ventilated roof was the machine shop. It measured 62.5 by 157 feet. The quarters for the troops are visible to the right. A lovely Greek Revival house is seen to the left. In photograph 7, Fort Morton is visible on the hilltop at the center, and one of the wheelright shops is to the right side of the machine shop. About 500 men were employed here. The ground plot explains the layout.* (NATIONAL ARCHIVES)

8. *The Tennessee barracks were somewhere in northwest Nashville between Spring and Broad streets. It consisted of eleven frame buildings measuring 230 by 24 feet each, and eighteen smaller ones used as troop quarters. The ground plot shows how these buildings were arranged.* (NATIONAL ARCHIVES)

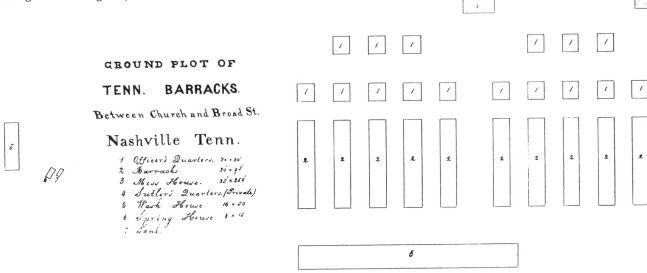

GROUND PLOT OF

TENN. BARRACKS.

Between Church and Broad St.

Nashville Tenn.

1 Officer's Quarters. 30'×20'
2 Barracks. 20'×95'
3 Mess House. 25'×250'
4 Sutler's Quarters (Private)
5 Wash House. 16×50
6 Spring House 8×15
7 Tank.

9. *The Nashville city tannery was just outside the corporation limits on Nolensville Pike east of Brown's Creek. It was the south's largest such facility prior to the war. A rail trestle and the smoking chimney of the tannery are in the distance in the middle of the photograph. Escaped slaves, contrabands working for the Federal army, are lined up for the photographer in the foreground.* (TENNESSEE STATE LIBRARY AND ARCHIVES)

10. *The post corral near the Murfreesboro Pike enclosed ten acres of land and included a forage house, stables, and quarters for the troops tending it. Only one horse is visible near the apparently long line of fodder at the center, since by this time the Federal army in the West was being organized for the* *invasion of Georgia and General Sherman had sent most of the troops, war materiel, medical supplies—and horses—to Chattanooga for the impending attack.* (NATIONAL ARCHIVES)

A MAGNIFICENT CAPITOL

I n the early nineteenth century, Tennessee had a roving capital. The legislature, governor, and the supreme court had officially met in Knoxville, Murfreesboro, Nashville, and Kingston at various times. Weary of its nomadic existence, the legislature voted in 1843 to make Nashville the permanent state capital. It was chosen because it was centrally located, on a navigable river, had a relatively large and urbane population—and because the town offered the state a gift of the top of the most prominent hill in town, Campbell's Hill, or Cedar Knob, for the new statehouse.

In January, 1844, commissioners were named to oversee the construction of the capitol and the selection and hiring of an architect. After a long search, they selected William Strickland in May, 1845, to serve as the on-site superintending architect. The cornerstone was laid with much ceremony on 4 July 1845. Although Ohio had a statehouse somewhat equal to Tennessee's under construction, no completed building outside Washington, D.C., could compare with it. It was the first building to be constructed in the United States, outside Washington, that used stonework on such a scale. People marvelled when they saw it.

William Strickland was born in Navesink, New Jersey, in 1788 and moved to Philadelphia at an early age. As an apprentice to Benjamin Henry Latrobe, the great Anglo-American architect, he helped build the United States Capitol in the new town of Washington, D.C. Returning to Philadelphia, Strickland won many commissions, designing the Delaware breakwater, St. Stephen's Church, the Second Bank of the United States, the tower on Independence Hall, and the Merchants Exchange. He was a founder of the American Institute of Architects and was one of the country's greatest architects at the time. Since the Panic of 1837 and the ensuing depression had caused a decline in large commissions in the east, Strickland was pleased to cap his distinguished career with so monumental a job as the Tennessee statehouse, a project which was to consume the rest of his life.

By the fall of 1853 construction of the capitol had advanced enough to allow the General Assembly to meet there. Six more years would pass, however, before it would be completed. To keep labor costs down, both convicts from the nearby state penitentiary and slaves were used. However, since they did not possess all the skills required for this massive project, others were hired to do such jobs as finished stone cutting, plastering, furniture making, painting, and glass making. In spite of efforts to economize, the money it took to build the capitol staggered the imaginations of the legislators. The total cost was $879,981.48.

On 7 April 1854 William Strickland died in the City Hotel where he lived. He was interred in a niche cut into the north portico, a high honor that is unusual in any building except churches, and a unique one for an architect in a capitol building. A few days before Strickland's death, the commissioners had unanimously elected Samuel D. Morgan to be chairman of the capitol commission, and on 3 June 1854 Strickland's oldest son, Francis, was named to succeed his father as the capitol's architect. He served in that capacity until he was dismissed on 1 May 1857, when the building had been enclosed entirely and the 205-foot-high tower had been completed. For the next nineteen months no architect was employed to supervise the work, and Morgan fulfilled that task himself. In 1880 he too was interred in the capitol, in its south portico. When it came time to finish the chamber for the state library, however, Harvey M. Akeroyd was hired, in December, 1858. This project was completed in time for the October legislative session in 1859. Landscaping was begun in 1860, but the growing secession crisis prevented the completion of the grounds prior to the war. Barnard's photographs show the beginning of the work on the retaining walls for the hill and of a rough grading for a promenade system.

Still in use as the Tennessee State Capitol, the building has seen the enfranchisement of blacks and women in its chambers and the coming and going of many generations of politicians. With its enormous stone-lined halls and chambers, it is as impressive today as it was in the nineteenth century. An Indiana soldier writing home in March, 1862 said that it "is the finest building I ever saw." Its awesome majesty continues to be a source of great pride to Tennesseans.

11. *The crowning jewel on the Nashville skyline is the capitol building, seen here from the north. The photographer, who is unknown, was on the roof of a Germantown house. The John H. Buddeke home is to the left, and the Church of the Assumption (Roman Catholic) is across Vine Street from it. When Assumption was built about 1859, Bishop Whelan referred to its location as "being far removed from Nashville." Notice the elevated rail trestle between Germantown and Nashville at the bottom of the hill on which Nashville sits. It was in the same area as the present elevated rail line. Notice also all of the exposed stone on the slope of Capitol Hill. This photograph was probably made in the late 1860s, but the town looked much like this in 1864.* (TENNESSEE STATE LIBRARY AND ARCHIVES)

12. *Fortifications and troop tents, as well as four brush arbors, are in the yard of the Tennessee State Capitol next to the construction office. The view here is that of the east, or main, facade. "Old Glory," Captain William Driver's ship flag, was flown from the pole above the main entrance on the day that Nashville was first occupied by the Union army in 1862.*

Driver was a New England sea captain who, when presented with a flag for his first ship, named it "Old Glory," thus coining a new sobriquet for the American flag. He settled in Nashville in 1837 and was a proud Unionist. When the War Between the States came along, it divided his family. Three sons served the Confederacy, while Captain Driver himself headed the war claims commission in Nashville during the occupation. (NATIONAL ARCHIVES)

13. *The eastern facade of the capitol is again seen here, facing the Cumberland River, nineteenth century Nashville's main commercial and passenger entry point. Barricades block the stairs at the main entrance, while horses are tied up at the south entrance.*

The tower of St. Mary's Church (Roman Catholic) is seen to the left. It looked as it does here until the architectural firm of Asmus and Clark renovated the structure in the 1920s and marred its beauty by removing its round clocks and the volutes, and by enclosing the bell chamber. (TENNESSEE STATE LIBRARY AND ARCHIVES)

14. *Nashville was literally a city under the gun during the Federal occupation, as seen here. Parrot guns were trained across the town from Capitol Hill and could send their projectiles one mile. The steeple of McKendree Methodist Church is at the left of the rusticated base of the capitol portico. It was at McKendree that the seditious Nashville Convention of 1850 was held to discuss southern secession. Between the lamp posts can be seen the twin towers of the old First Presbyterian Church. Somewhat obscured by a tree is the hip-roofed St. Cloud Hotel, situated diagonally across Spring Street from First Presbyterian Church. At various times during the war, Andrew Johnson, Military Governor of Tennessee, and General George Thomas were guests of the hotel. The Masonic Hall is at the left of the twin-towered church and the Maxwell House hotel at its left. At the left are the twin Gothic spires of the First Baptist Church. This view looks southeast. This, and the accompanying 1986 view, are both from the ledge on the east side of the capitol's north portico.* (LIBRARY OF CONGRESS, J.A.H.)

[14A]

[15A]

15. *The northeastern view from the main entrance to the capitol shows the Cumberland River on the right. The dirt track leading off to the left is High Street. Behind the lamp at the right is seen the rear of Hynes High School on Line Street, at the corner of Summer Street. This and the accompanying 1986 view are both from the ledge on the east side of the capitol's south portico.* (NATIONAL ARCHIVES, J.A.H.)

16. *The west facade is seen here behind a tree. Horses are tethered on the south side of the capitol, and a ladder is leaned against a lamp post. Perhaps dusk is approaching.* (PHOTOGRAPH BY CARL C. GIERS FROM THE COLLECTION OF HERB PECK)

17. *The view from the north portico, looking southwest, shows Vine Street opposite the capitol. The clapboard house occupies part of the site of today's Supreme Court Building, which is shown in the accompanying 1986 view.* (LIBRARY OF CONGRESS, J.A.H.)

[17A]

18. *This is the same view from the north portico of the capitol as photograph 17, except that it has rained and the cannons and caisson are covered with tarpaulins to protect them. The air has cleared somewhat. More clearly visible is Polk Place, the home of President and Mrs. James K. Polk, seen just to the right of the tree behind the left lamppost. The clapboard house to the right is seen again in photographs 17 and 19.* (LIBRARY OF CONGRESS)

[19]   [20]

19–20. *It is thought that the civilians standing by the clapboard house on Vine Street looking to the southwest are listening to the rolling thunder of the cannon, musket, and rifle fire of the Battle of Nashville. They could easily have seen the smoke of the battle rising from the hills to the south of town. The Battle of Nashville, which took place on 15 and 16 December 1864, was a crushing Union victory. The factory at the center of the photograph is a railroad repair shop built in the rail yards by the Federal army to enable it to equip, transport, and communicate with the troops moving out from Nashville into Georgia to conquer the South. The photographer is unknown.* (LIBRARY OF CONGRESS)

21. *This is the railroad repair shop as it appeared while under construction in the valley west of the capitol. The lantern tower of the capitol is visible to the right of the smoke stack.* (NATIONAL ARCHIVES)

[22A]

22. *The south portico of the capitol clearly shows the cotton bales, wooden palisades, and earthworks which had transformed it into Fort Andrew Johnson prior to 1864. The front of the capitol (east side) is to the right.*

The masonry and stone wall in the foreground are along High Street. This and the 1986 view are both taken from High Street (Sixth Avenue) near Cedar Street (Charlotte Avenue). (NATIONAL ARCHIVES, J.A.H.)

23. *Trees and lamps are reflected in rainwater puddles on the upper terrace to the south portico of the capitol, seen here looking west. The gas lamps on the stair piers are graced by three cast iron allegorical figures, representing morning, noon, and night. The gas burners are clearly visible within these lamps made by Wood and Perrot of Philadelphia. Eight of these beautiful lamps adorned the capitol, two at each of the entrance stairs.* (TENNESSEE STATE LIBRARY AND ARCHIVES)

24. *The rainwater has evaporated, and the same dapper fellow is seen lounging against a lamppost in this view of the south portico steps looking east. Just to the left of the farthest lamp is the Davidson County Courthouse and city market. The capitol construction office is on the front grounds of the just completed capitol, to the left at the end of the upper terrace.* (LIBRARY OF CONGRESS)

[25A]

25. *The view from the north portico of the capitol shows a broad open field beyond the loopholed palisade and earthwork. The first road to the left is Vine Street; High Street is to the right. The large building on the left of Vine Street, in the distance, is the Church of the Assumption.* (TENNESSEE HISTORICAL SOCIETY, J.A.H.)

RAILROADS IN NASHVILLE

When Nashville's first locomotive arrived in December, 1850, it had to come on a steamboat because no rail lines had been built to Nashville yet. At the time, it was little understood how important the event was.

In 1851 the engine made its first run to Antioch, a trip of eleven miles. By 1854, however, Nashville was tied to Chattanooga by rail and from there to the Atlantic seaboard. Goods from Europe or New York could be shipped to Savannah or Charleston for rail delivery to Nashville. Finished goods such as cloth or furniture could be ordered from any of the world's major market places and shipped to Nashville at unheard of speed and with little chance of loss or damage. Nashvillians could enjoy the latest fashions as seen in *Godey's Lady's Book* or *Harper's* and could decorate their homes in the most up-to-date manner. Farmers could order the newest "improved" implements. Manufacturers could have the latest innovations in machinery shipped to them. Even mail delivery was expedited. Railroads transformed Middle Tennessee.

In 1859 the Louisville and Nashville line opened, giving Nashville greater access to the Great Lakes area. In 1853 and 1854, the Nashville and Decatur line was built south to the Tennessee River. From Decatur rail lines also ran west to Memphis. From Chattanooga other rail lines ran to Knoxville and the Valley of Virginia. The War Between the States was the first time when railroads were used extensively by the military. The Federal army, with more miles of track available and a larger industrial base than the Confederacy, was prepared to exploit to the fullest advantage the possibilities that railroads had in warfare. They could carry troops into the field and bring the wounded and dead back home. They could be used to ship men, pack and saddle animals, livestock, food, munitions, wagons, fodder, food, medical supplies, doctors, and armaments to and from the combat fronts.

However, railroads were costly to build and maintain. Enormous effort went into repairing enemy-damaged trestles, engines, and rolling stock as well as into constructing warehouses to handle the materiel needed to keep the troops in the field. The old roundhouse in Nashville was found to be too small for the needs of wartime traffic, and so the military demolished it and built a larger repair shop. Nashville was transformed into a great supply center, and the river and rail links that Nashville enjoyed enabled the Federal army to supply itself for the assault on Murfreesboro and ultimately against Chattanooga, Atlanta, Savannah, and the Carolinas.

All of the rail lines in Union-controlled Tennessee were put to the exclusive use of the military. The track, equipment, supplies, and rolling stock were all seized for the war effort. When John Hunt Morgan's men blew up the rail tunnel north of Nashville in 1862, the military resumed work abandoned earlier on a rail line to the west to by-pass this northern bottleneck. The Nashville and Northwestern railroad was extended to Johnsonville on the Tennessee River, where an enormous warehouse depot was built. It was substantially complete by May of 1864. Later in 1864 Nathan Bedford Forrest raided this depot and destroyed more than two million dollars worth of United States property.

Although during the war railroad assets were used to conquer the South, after the war the Louisville and Nashville and the other regional lines reacquired their equipment and used it to build a new South.

26. *The remarkable engineering of Nashville's swing-span railroad bridge, built in the 1850s, is seen in this 1864 photograph. The center span could be pivoted to permit riverboats with tall smokestacks to pass through. Also visible are the fortifications built onto the bridge's superstructure by the Federal authorities who were fearful of the dangerous Confederate raiders led* by John Hunt Morgan and Nathan Bedford Forrest. Both had made raids near Nashville in 1862, and, on one occasion, Morgan had burned a Union steamboat at the wharf. (T.M. SCHLEIER PHOTOGRAPH FROM THE COLLECTION OF HERB PECK)

[28]

[27]

27–28. *These views of the swing-span railroad bridge over the Cumberland River show the guard turrets, gates with loopholes, and sentries guarding this vital link into the town. Photograph 28 was taken from below the span.* (TENNESSEE HISTORICAL SOCIETY AND LIBRARY OF CONGRESS)

[29]

[30]

29. *The master mechanic's office had an ornamental bell tower on top of it. Contrabands, refugee slaves who had escaped from their owners, are to the right. At the left, a repair shop is being built west of the capitol. The shop was used to repair the railroad's rolling stock.* (NATIONAL ARCHIVES)

30. *The brick building at the left was a church for blacks prior to the war. The military seized it during the occupation and converted it into a brass shop. The wooden structures in the foreground were copper shops, which were in the rail yard west of the capitol. Train parts lie about the yard. The repair shop smokestack is seen above the roof of the copper shop.* (NATIONAL ARCHIVES)

31. *The Nashville and Chattanooga rail yard was situated near Spring Street, which extends through the valley behind the photographer. The capitol looks down upon the scene. Thirteen engines fill the rail yard.* (TENNESSEE HISTORICAL SOCIETY)

32. *Supply houses stored food, clothing, and ammunition necessary for the Federal troops stationed in Nashville and in the field of war. This supply house was situated in the rail yard west of the capitol.* (NATIONAL ARCHIVES)

33. *When the Federal army took over the railroads in Nashville, it added a printing office (at the right) to the passenger depot (on the left). For scale, note the man standing between the windows of the depot.* (NATIONAL ARCHIVES)

[34]

[35]

34–35. *These two photographs show the rail yard. Spring Street is visible on the right where the Church Street viaduct now spans the valley. The building on the left has been whitewashed in photograph 35. In the earlier photo the back of Polk Place is seen above the roof of the central building, between the two hip-roofed buildings. The millwork on the eaves is very elaborate in the rail building to the right. The later photograph shows a market set up beside the tracks. Slave women are apparently selling produce.* (NATIONAL ARCHIVES)

36. *The rail yard for the Nashville and Chattanooga line was situated north of Spring Street in the valley that the railroad still uses today. During the war the Federal authorities greatly expanded the usage and size of the rail yard and its shops. In this photograph at least eighteen engines are visible.* *The castellated Gothic passenger station is at the right. The scaffolding in the center is an indication that the old roundhouse was being demolished and a new repair shop was being built in its place. That shop was seen from Capitol Hill in photographs 19–20.* (NATIONAL ARCHIVES)

[37]

[38]

37–38–39. *The government stables and mess house in the rail yard area were north of the Nashville and Chattanooga terminal. The capitol tower is visible in photograph 37, and the back of Polk Place in photographs 38 and 39. Water runs in the horse trough from the pump.* (NATIONAL ARCHIVES)

[39]

40. *This stable yard for the post ambulances appears to have been near the medical complex around the Shelby Medical College. The valley through which the railroad ran is visible to the left.* (NATIONAL ARCHIVES)

41. *This forage house measured 60 by 180 feet and was used to store food for either man or beast. Captain Jonathan F. Isom, assistant quartermaster, had overseen its construction. Its location is unknown.* (NATIONAL ARCHIVES)

42. *As the war progressed, Nashville became the chief supply depot for the Federal army in the western theater. More and more rolling stock was processed through the town as troops, medicines, munitions, and supplies were sent south to provision the Federal army as it fought its way to the Atlantic.* (NATIONAL ARCHIVES)

43. *The Nashville coal yard had a capacity of four million bushels.* (NATIONAL ARCHIVES)

[44]

44–45. *The Taylor Depot was a commissary warehouse for food supplies built near the end of the Tennessee and Alabama Railroad, at the corner of Summer and Broad streets. Photograph 44 shows the side of the building fronting the railroad. In the distance, from left to right, are the towers of Christ Episcopal, McKendree Methodist, and First Presbyterian churches. Photograph 45 is a panoramic view in which two plates fit together to show the south side (left) and rear (right) views of the Taylor Depot. This building burned down on 9 June 1865. Prior to the war, the Tennessee and Alabama Depot had been located on the south side of Broad Street, midway between Cherry and Summer streets.* (NATIONAL ARCHIVES AND TENNESSEE HISTORICAL SOCIETY)

[45]

[46]

[46A]

46-47-48. *Like the Taylor Depot, the Eaton Depot was used to store war materiel and was situated in south Nashville along the rail lines running south of the Nashville and Chattanooga Depot. It was astride High Street (see the ground plot). Photograph 46 shows some of the houses in the area at the right. Also visible, from right to left, are the Ensley Building, the court house, the Market House, the Maxwell House hotel, the Masonic Hall, First Presbyterian Church, McKendree Methodist Church, Christ Episcopal Church, and the capitol. The tower on Holy Trinity (Episcopal) Church is not visible because it was not completed until sometime after 1887. Photograph 47 shows Fort Negley to the right. Photograph 48 shows the addition of more warehouse space while the depot was still under construction.* (NATIONAL ARCHIVES, J.A.H.)

[47]

[47A]

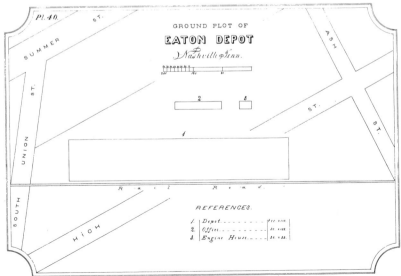

UP ON COLLEGE HILL

The University of Nashville was a source of particular pride in prewar Nashville. The school was an outgrowth of Davidson Academy, the first school established in the frontier settlement. Founded in 1785 north of Nashville near the present-day National Cemetery on Gallatin Road, it relocated in 1802 on 240 acres that an 1801 Tennessee legislative act had set aside south of Broad Street "for the promotion of learning in Davidson County." This area became known later as "College Hill."

The little school made modest progress under the Reverend Thomas B. Craighead and Dr. James Priestly, but when Dr. Philip Lindsley became president in 1825, a period of real growth and distinction began. Dr. Lindsley had declined the presidency of Princeton University to come to Nashville. In 1826 the institution's name was changed to the University of Nashville. With the infusion of funds from the George Peabody trust in 1875, the school became the Peabody Normal College, a teacher training school. In 1906 its name was changed to the George Peabody College for Teachers, and in 1914 the school moved across town to a location near the campus of Vanderbilt University. In 1979 it was merged with Vanderbilt.

By 1851 the need for larger facilities at the university had been recognized, and so an expansion of the medical college was begun under the architectural direction of Adolphus Heiman who completed a Greek Revival-style building for the school in 1854. The medical college was then situated on a block bordered by Market, College, Priestly, and Franklin streets. Fashionable condominiums now occupy the site. The expansion occurred during the early years of the presidency of John Berrien Lindsley, son of Philip Lindsley. When the war reached Nashville, the Confederates took over the university to quarter troops and to use it as a hospital. Through Lindsley's efforts, the medical college remained open for instruction throughout the war.

The main campus of the university was at the top of College Hill, facing Market Street and extending back toward University Street, where the Montgomery Bell Academy property later adjoined it. Toward the northwest corner stood a Federal-style building that housed the faculty living quarters, a commissary, infirmary, and dining hall. Behind it, but separated from it, stood the steam plant. At the northeast end of the complex stood Lindsley Hall. Just south of the steam plant, in 1853–54, Heiman erected the Literary Department building, a structure which still stands and is used as the offices for the Metro Planning Commission. When the cost of constructing the Literary Department building proved to be more than the school could bear, it initiated into its instructional program in 1855 the classes of a tuition-generating military school called the Western Military Institute.

The university attracted a number of prominent people as professors, including Dr. Gerard Troost, the state geologist, and Dr. Augustin Gattinger. Colonel Bushrod Rust Johnson—who later became a general in the Confederate army—and Colonel Richard Owen were added to the faculty when it merged with Western Military Institute.

Prominent neighbors of the university were Henry Middleton Rutledge and his wife, Septima Sexta Rutledge. The Rutledges had moved to Middle Tennessee from South Carolina in the 1820s and lived at Chilhowee for a time before moving to Nashville and settling upon College Hill on property they named Rose Hill. Like Middleton Place, Mrs. Rutledge's home near Charleston, Rose Hill was laid out with a central square block and flanking wings. Descending the hill, it had terraced gardens stepping down toward a bend in the Cumberland River and to the Lebanon Turnpike. Unfortunately no photographs of the house have been found, but the 1860 Haydon and Booth map of Nashville and Edgefield does show its outline. The house burned sometime near the end of the war and only part of a flanking wing survives.

From 1850 to 1854 South Nashville was incorporated as a separate town, but in 1854 it merged with Nashville. Strong community feeling survived, however. Later Howard School was a focal point there for South Nashville, and several Protestant churches on College Hill added to the sense of community. Methodists, Baptists, Presbyterians, Episcopalians, and Primitive Baptists all worshiped on the hill, their churches close to each other.

[49]

[49]

[49A]

[49B]

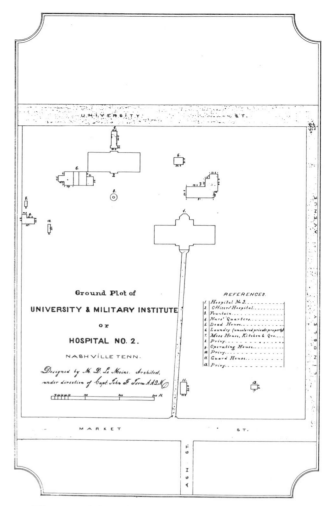

49. *Three photographs taken from the roof of Lindsley Hall form a panoramic view of the campus of the University of Nashville. The map of the campus was made by the Federal army. The Literary Department building of the university is at the left. Today it houses the Metropolitan Nashville/Davidson County Planning Commission. The architect's plans for this building, which included an elaborate Gothic Revival tower for the center and flanking wings, were never fully realized, as the University's chronic cash shortages never allowed either to be built. Notice the man standing on the roof.*

Beyond this building lies South Market Street, screened here by a whitewashed plank fence. The large three-story brick factory building with the tall smokestack is the College Hill Armory. A one-story wing projects to the west from it. Fort Negley crowns the hill beyond and at the left. It is more visible in photograph 49A.

The rear of the university faculty housing is seen at the right. Beyond its rooftop and at the right is the tower of Howard School. The large brick structure with white pilasters at the far right is the medical college.

The center section of this panoramic view shows three College Hill churches. Two are back to back along Elm Street. An unidentified church on Summer Street is capped by a beautiful steeple, seen most clearly in photograph 49B. The Cherry Street Baptist Church faces the photographer behind two trees, to the left of the professors' housing. Both the Cherry Street Baptist Church and the Primitive Baptist Church, seen through the trees to the left of the chimneys of the faculty housing, are shown again in photographs 59 and 60. (LIBRARY OF CONGRESS)

50. *George Barnard used the roof of Lindsley Hall as a platform for his camera in taking this photograph of the town of Nashville to the north. The capitol, First Presbyterian Church, and the Cumberland River are visible.* (LIBRARY OF CONGRESS)

51. *This building at the corner of Castleman and Guthrie streets appears to have been a factory. It was a brick building with a wooden shingle roof and measured 40 by 68 feet. The post teamsters (wagoners) used it as their quarters. Their blankets are being aired on the windowsills. The openable skylights are a striking feature. The building is also visible in photograph* 50. (NATIONAL ARCHIVES)

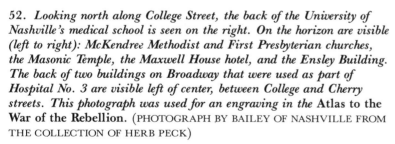

52. *Looking north along College Street, the back of the University of Nashville's medical school is seen on the right. On the horizon are visible (left to right): McKendree Methodist and First Presbyterian churches, the Masonic Temple, the Maxwell House hotel, and the Ensley Building. The back of two buildings on Broadway that were used as part of Hospital No. 3 are visible left of center, between College and Cherry streets. This photograph was used for an engraving in the* Atlas to the War of the Rebellion. (PHOTOGRAPH BY BAILEY OF NASHVILLE FROM THE COLLECTION OF HERB PECK)

53. *Looking down Market Street from College Hill, the eastern wing of the medical college is on the left and the capitol and the First Presbyterian Church are on the skyline. The Brennan Foundry is on the waterfront on Front Street, beside the city wharf. The Broad Street Fire Company No. 2 is visible in the center, as well as an 1850s building that still survives at 210 Broadway.* (TENNESSEE STATE MUSEUM COLLECTION)

54. *Housing for the president and other staff of the University of Nashville was used by the Federal army as a part of Hospital No. 2. Dr. Philip Lindsley lived here. The building was made of brick, had a wooden shingle roof, and measured 94 by 172 feet. These architectural drawings show the floor plan and how the various segments used by the other staff members were connected by doorways. The building was on the northwest corner of the university property. The long ell at the back contained a dining hall, kitchen, store, laundry, and shops. It was added in 1855 and was heated by the university steam plant, seen at the extreme right.* (NATIONAL ARCHIVES)

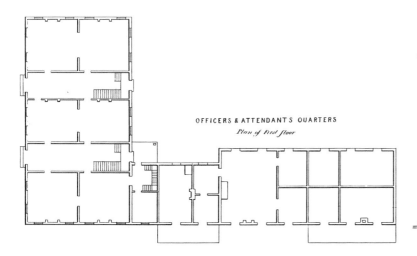

OFFICERS & ATTENDANTS QUARTERS
Plan of First floor

55. *The Literary Department building was constructed between 1853 and 1854 at a cost of $45,000. The undercapitalized university could not make a go of this department, however, and it closed in 1855. This building then housed the Western Military Institute run by Colonels Bushrod Johnson and Richard Owen. All of the cadets entered the Confederate service at the outbreak of hostilities. One cadet, Sam Davis, was hanged in 1863 by the Federal army for treason as a Confederate spy. Following the war, Generals Bushrod Johnson and Edmund Kirby-Smith ran the school for five years.*

The building was made of limestone, had a composition roof, and measured 175 by 50 feet. As a Federal hospital attached to Hospital No. 2, it had 300 beds. The floor plans show that one entire room was set aside for "dead-men's knapsacks." During the war there were more deaths from sickness and surgery than there were on the battlefield. Yet it was in this war, at Shiloh, that the first field hospital was employed. (NATIONAL ARCHIVES)

FRONT-ELEVATION.

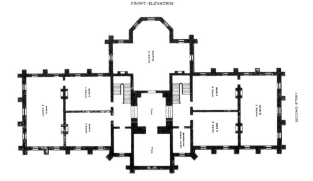

56. *The University of Nashville's Lindsley Hall was built in 1855 and was probably designed by Adolphus Heiman. It was used both by the Confederate and Federal armies as a military hospital. This three-story building was made of brick, had a composition roof, and measured 152 by 56 feet. As a Federal hospital it contained 200 beds and was reserved for officers. Like many other hospital buildings, the foundations had a lime-based whitewash applied to them in the belief that it helped to prevent "contagion." A similar practice of whitewashing the base of trees is still sometimes seen in rural areas.*

In recent years this building has been confused with the surviving Literary Department building, which is a two-story limestone structure. The confusion has gone so far that the Metro Council has even formally renamed the Literary Department building "Lindsley Hall." The actual Lindsley Hall was built as a dormitory. The floor plans were created for a Sanitary Commission report on the building.

The University steam plant is visible to the left. All of the buildings were heated by it, according to the 1860–61 **City Directory.** (NATIONAL ARCHIVES)

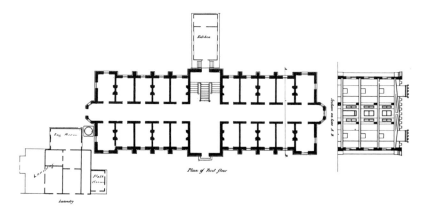

[57]

[58]

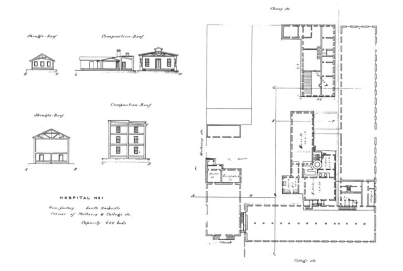

57. *Identified by Federal authorities as a Methodist church, the building in the foreground was actually the Third Presbyterian Church, situated at the corner of Mulberry and College streets. It stood south of the College Hill Armory, seen behind it. The church measured 48 by 72 feet and had a wooden shingle roof. Along with the armory, it was Hospital No. 1, Division 2. The armory was a brick building also and measured 176 by 48 feet. An adjoining one-story brick building was 240 by 48 feet. These three structures together had a bed capacity of 650. The accompanying cross sectional diagrams and floor plan show the interior of both the church and the College Hill Armory.* (NATIONAL ARCHIVES)

58. *The College Hill Armory and the Third Presbyterian Church are cordoned off with chevaux-de-frise, obstacles of pointed sticks buried in the ground with the sharp ends pointing toward advancing enemy troops. Written on the back of this print is a description of this defensive measure as ". . . the last line of defense against Hood's army when it was besieging Nashville & Thomas, Dec. 1864." The painting of the addition at the rear of the church has been completed.* (PHOTOGRAPHER UNKNOWN. FROM THE COLLECTION OF HERB PECK)

59. *The Primitive Baptist Church on College Street, built in 1850, was a brick building with a wooden shingle roof. Used by the Federal army in conjunction with Hospital No. 1, it contained sixty beds. The church was greatly altered later as can be seen in the present-day photograph.* (NATIONAL ARCHIVES, J.A.H.)

[59A]

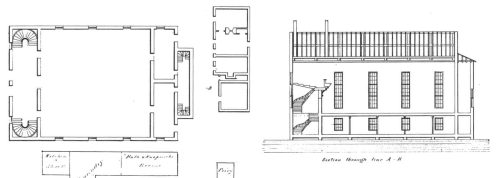

60. *At the corner of Elm and Cherry streets, the Cherry Street Baptist Church (built in 1858–59) was used as the post hospital. It was made of brick, had a wooden shingle roof, measured 58 by 92 feet, and contained 125 beds. Most Nashville churches were seized by the military during the occupation.* (NATIONAL ARCHIVES)

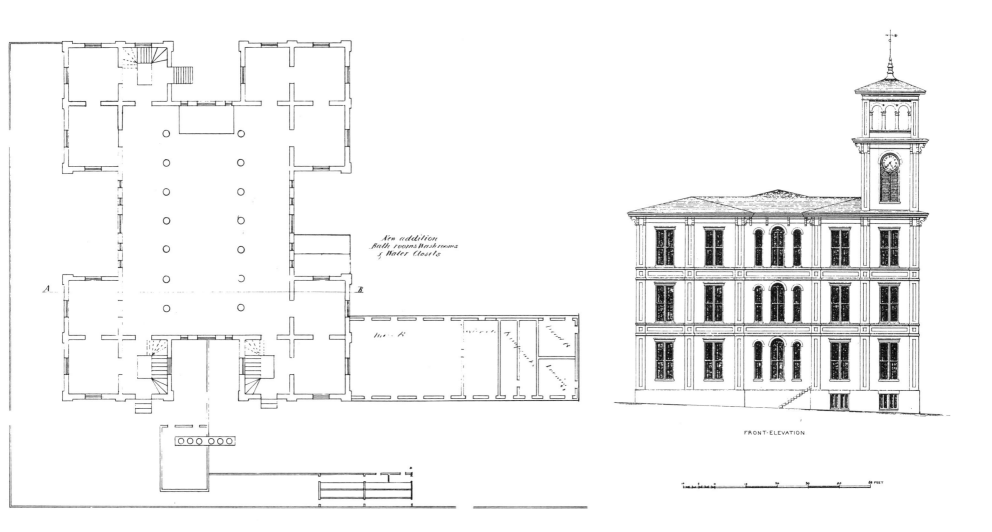

61. *Howard School was built on College Street in 1860 by Harvey M. Akeroyd on land deeded in 1859 by Memican Hunt Howard to the city of Nashville for a public school. It was brick with a wooden shingle roof and measured 94 by 110 feet. The floor plans show a large central room on each floor with smaller rooms in the corners and an elaborate Italianate clock tower, as Mr. Howard had stipulated that the building have "a large, good clock with a suitable loud-tones bell announcing the hours." This Howard School was located northwest of the present building of that same name.* (NATIONAL ARCHIVES)

[62A]

62. *The Elm Street Methodist Church still stands on the corner of Elm Street and Summer Street. Today, however, it is without a steeple and the Lafayette Street extension runs through the site of these barracks. The 1986 photograph shows these changes.* (PHOTOGRAPH BY T. M. SCHLEIER FROM THE COLLECTION OF HERB PECK, J.A.H.)

63. *This College Hill residence stood at the corner of Mulberry and College streets. It was brick, had a wooden shingle roof, and measured 40 by 30 feet. It was used in connection with Hospital No. 1.* (NATIONAL ARCHIVES)

64. *On a corner lot on College Hill, this Federal-style townhouse was used in connection with Hospital No. 1. Eight boys stand or sit on the back fence. A soldier, another boy, two white women, and a black are in the front yard, all posing for the photographer.* (NATIONAL ARCHIVES)

65. *Also used in connection with Hospital No. 1, this College Hill home grew with its owners. It began as a simple Federal-style house with a side hall. A pair of flanking rooms was added to the right side, converting it into a two-room-over-two-room, central-hall house. An animal head hangs on the chimney wall nearest the photographer.* (NATIONAL ARCHIVES)

A CITY OF BEAUTIFUL ARCHITECTURE

I ascend to the cupola of the magnificent statehouse in Nashville, and survey the surrounding country. On every side spread the broadly undulating fields and hills into the illimitable distance. . . . A more beautiful landscape diversified with broad clearings, waving crops, tufts of poplar and magnolia, shining mansions, withdrawing vales, and purple atmosphere, it has never been my privilege to see.

Alexander Winchell wrote this in 1870 in his "Sketches of Creation," but it would have described Nashville prior to the war as well.

The first brick homes built in Nashville were erected about 1800, and by the time of the War Between the States most of the houses were constructed of masonry. This gave the city a substantial and fixed appearance. Nashville was a town that had entertained Louis Philippe in his exile during the turmoil of the French Revolution and the Directory, had celebrated the later visit of the Marquis de Lafayette, and was the home of two recent presidents. The widow of President Polk still lived in their townhouse and was visited regularly by the most distinguished visitors to the city. A future president, Andrew Johnson, was also living in Nashville, heading the military government.

The architecture of the homes was primarily of Federal style, but the latest trends were also to be found: Gothic Revival, Greek Revival, and the Italianate style. David Morrison, one of the earliest prominent architects in Nashville, probably designed the Davidson County Courthouse in 1829 and is known to have been responsible for the State Penitentiary in 1830, the Tennessee State Hospital for the Insane (later Nashville City Hospital) in 1833, and McKendree Methodist Church also in 1833.

Adolphus Heiman, a Prussian-born architect, followed Morrison in the 1830s as the leading local architect and continued to work until the War Between the States. He designed St. Mary's Catholic Church, the new Tennessee State Hospital for the Insane, Hume School, the academic buildings at the University of Nashville, First Baptist Church, the Masonic Hall, and Belmont, the Acklen mansion. During the latter years of his career, Heiman worked in competition for commissions.

Harvey Akeroyd, an English immigrant, came to Nashville during the 1840s and designed the Hicks and Ensley buildings on the Public Square, as well as Howard School, St. Cecilia Academy, and the Tennessee State Library chamber in the capitol.

William Strickland came to Nashville from Philadelphia in 1845 to design and oversee the construction of the state capitol building. While in Nashville, he also designed the First (now Downtown) Presbyterian Church and the Wilson County Courthouse. He apparently also designed Second Presbyterian Church. His son, Francis, designed the 1857 Davidson County Courthouse, the Bank of Tennessee, and finished most of the structural work on the capitol.

All of these architects made Nashville a city of beautiful architecture, each working in his own way with styles that best suited his own techniques and taste. Morrison's forte was Federal style; Heiman's was Gothic, classical, and Italianate; while Akeroyd's was primarily Italianate. William Strickland preferred Greek Revival, with one flamboyant exception, the Egyptian-influenced First Presbyterian Church. His son, Francis, was noted for his classical style with some Italianate detailing. The beauty of tree shaded, architecturally diverse Nashville was even appreciated by its conquerors, who largely spared its buildings—and people—from the destruction of war.

The many large farms and estates around Nashville were particularly impressive. In May of 1862 an Ohio soldier, writing to his sister, described Belmont, Joseph Acklen's home.

His house is a palace and the yard in front is filled with flowers and plants of every description, magnolia trees and marble statues of every kind. Besides the marble there are figures of Negroes dancing, and dogs, lion, deer, and I don't know what all, laying around amongst the shrubbery. Beside a great many kinds of flowers in the yard he has two greenhouses filled with flowers and plants from all parts of the world.

Another Federal soldier described the grounds glowingly as looking "like a first-class cemetery." The profusion of statues and plantings did give it this appearance, for in those days public parks were nearly unknown and such an abundance of plants and statuary was seen by most people only in cemeteries.

When the nuns from St. Cecilia visited Belmont with their charges on a wartime excursion, Mother Frances Walsh said that "on viewing the vista that opened up from the grand avenue, thoughts of villas near the seven-hilled city or gorgeous scenes in the vicinity of Paris arose in the mind, so unexpected was it to see such a place in a new country, in a democracy." The girls of St. Cecilia Academy also had a wartime picnic at Belle Meade. Again, Mother Frances wrote, "To visitors, Nashville was second to Belle Meade. Its fine stock, deer park, its five or six thousand acres of woodland and cultivation artistically intermingled, had a national reputation."

Unfortunately no prewar photographs of the country estates are known to exist. But Barnard did photograph some of Nashville's homes that had been seized by the military. There are dignified Federal-style structures as well as the more flamboyant Italianate palazzo style of the Cunningham house and the eclectic Zollicoffer home. In short, the town had style and taste, and these attributes were reflected in its architecture.

STREET NAMES

The names of many of the streets in downtown Nashville have changed between the 1860s and now. Below is a list of both the previous names and the corresponding modern names. Throughout this book the older names will be used unless a reference is made to the modern street itself.

1860s	Today
BROAD STREET	BROADWAY
CASTLEMAN STREET	PEABODY STREET (between Second Avenue and the Cumberland River)
CEDAR STREET	CHARLOTTE AVENUE
CHERRY STREET	FOURTH AVENUE
CLARK STREET	BANK STREET
COLLEGE STREET	THIRD AVENUE
CUMBERLAND ALLEY	COMMERCE STREET
FRONT STREET	FIRST AVENUE (South of the Square)
GUTHRIE	No longer exists; the MTA Operations Center is now on the site
HIGH STREET	SIXTH AVENUE
LINE STREET	JO JOHNSTON STREET (between Third and Twenty-First avenues)
LOCUST STREET	JO JOHNSTON STREET (between First and Third avenues)
MARKET STREET	SECOND AVENUE
MCLEMORE STREET	NINTH AVENUE
MULBERRY STREET	SIXTEENTH AVENUE
PRIESTLEY STREET	PEABODY STREET (between Second and Fourth avenues)
SPRING STREET	CHURCH STREET
SPRUCE STREET	EIGHTH AVENUE
SUMMER STREET	FIFTH AVENUE
UNION ALLEY	UNION STREET
VINE STREET	SEVENTH AVENUE
WATER STREET	FIRST AVENUE (North of the Square)
WILLIAMS STREET	SEVENTEENTH AVENUE

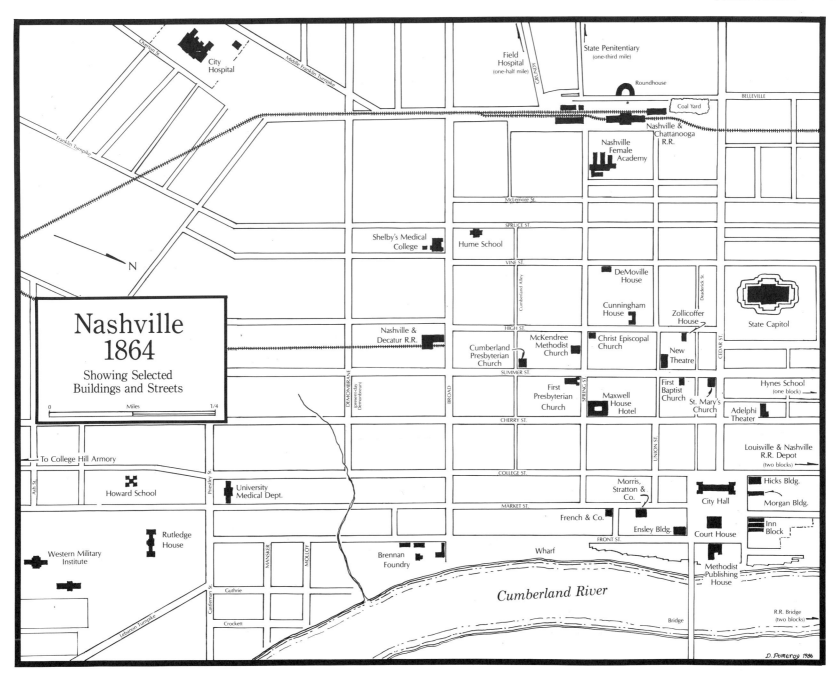

Nashville 1864

Showing Selected Buildings and Streets

0   Miles   1/4

N

City Hospital

State Penitentiary (one-third mile)

Field Hospital (one-half mile)

Roundhouse

BELLEVILLE

Coal Yard

Nashville & Chattanooga R.R.

Nashville Female Academy

McLemore St.

SPRUCE ST.

Shelby's Medical College

Hume School

VINE ST.

DeMoville House

Cumberland Alley

Cunningham House

Zollicoffer House

State Capitol

HIGH ST.

Nashville & Decatur R.R.

Cumberland Presbyterian Church

McKendree Methodist Church

Christ Episcopal Church

New Theatre

SUMMER ST.

First Presbyterian Church

Maxwell House Hotel

First Baptist Church

St. Mary's Church

Hynes School (one block)

Adelphi Theater

CHERRY ST.

Louisville & Nashville R.R. Depot (two blocks)

COLLEGE ST.

Morris, Stratton & Co.

Hicks Bldg.

City Hall

Morgan Bldg.

To College Hill Armory

Howard School

University Medical Dept.

MARKET ST.

French & Co.

Ensley Bldg.

Court House

Inn Block

Rutledge House

Western Military Institute

MANSKER

MOLLOY

Brennan Foundry

FRONT ST.

Wharf

Methodist Publishing House

Castleman St.

Guthrie

Crockett

Lebanon Turnpike

Cumberland River

Bridge

R.R. Bridge (two blocks)

Overton St.

Middle Franklin Turnpike

Franklin Turnpike

GROUND

Priestley St.

Ash St.

DEMOMBRANE (present-day Demonbreun)

BROAD

SPRING ST.

UNION ST.

Deaderick St.

CEDAR ST.

D. Pomeroy 1986

66. *General Miller's headquarters was situated somewhere on College Street in this very fashionable townhouse. The catchment to the roof guttering has the same Federal eagle, stars, and crescent moon on it that the Hermitage, the home of Andrew Jackson, drainage system has. Notice that the lower section of the downspout on the left side is missing. The ashlar foundation, the stone entrance way, the window lintels, and the string courses are very elegant, as is the gatepost at the right. But the most stylish feature of the house is the use of painted window shades upstairs. They appear to have geometrical borders with a landscaped center medallion. The owners evidently wanted their neighbors to see their good taste because the images are reversed so that they are visible from the exterior. The sidewalks are stone, as are the curb and gutters. A stone slab across the gutter allows unimpeded access to the house. This brick dwelling had a wooden shingle roof and measured 32 by 56 feet.* (NATIONAL ARCHIVES)

67. *This transitional Federal/Greek-revival townhouse was near the Louisville & Nashville railroad and was used by Federal authorities to house rail employees. It was of brick construction, had a wooden shingle roof, and measured 54 by 36 feet. The rude plank fencing was typical in this period. Above the door is painted "Erected A.D. 1842."* (NATIONAL ARCHIVES)

[68]

68. *This Cherry Street double row house was next to an alley. Someone stands in the doorway to the left, and houseplants are taking in the sunlight on the windowsill upstairs. The Assistant Medical Director of the Federal army used these homes as an office. They were brick with a wooden shingle roof and measured 28 by 40 feet.* (NATIONAL ARCHIVES)

69. *This double row house on Cherry Street was used as the Chief Quartermaster's office. It was constructed of brick, had a wooden shingle roof, and measured 96 by 42 feet. Long exposure times caused the blurring of objects that moved in these early photographs. Most of the men are moving in this image as is the enormous American flag hanging on a pole from the third floor window of the house at the corner. The two women with a child crossing the street on the right are also blurred.* (NATIONAL ARCHIVES)

70. *Two of the assistant quartermasters used these double row houses, which also stood on Cherry Street, as their offices. The buildings were made of brick, had wooden shingle roofs, and measured 60 by 42 feet each. The neighbors could not decide upon a common treatment of the jointly used structure. The right half has been painted and has had window awnings added to two floors. Stables appear to be on both sides of the property.* (NATIONAL ARCHIVES)

71. *A Captain Little, the Assistant Commissary of Subsistence, used this Cherry Street residence as his office. Behind the sycamore trees, a raised gallery overlooks the street. Neoclassical ornamentation highlights the detailing. The home was made of brick, had a composition roof, and measured 28 by 42 feet.* (NATIONAL ARCHIVES)

[69]

[70]

[71]

72. *Swiss immigrant Felix Zollicoffer lived in this townhouse on High Street, where the Polk Center stands today. Zollicoffer, who was killed in battle at Fishing Creek, Kentucky, was the first Confederate general to die in the western theater. The building measured 32 by 48 feet, and was used by Federal authorities as the Provost Marshal's office. A door from it survives in a Nashville home.* (NATIONAL ARCHIVES)

73. *The George W. Cunningham house on High Street, where the Capitol Boulevard Building stands today, was a very elegant Renaissance-Revival dwelling. When Barnard photographed it, General Sherman was using it as his headquarters. Other Federal commanders who used it were Don Carlos Buell, William S. Rosecrans, Ulysses S. Grant, and George H. Thomas. Rosecrans's chief of staff was James A. Garfield. The brick building had a composition roof and measured 42 by 56 feet. Later the Hermitage Club occupied it and added a third floor. It was razed around 1930.* (NATIONAL ARCHIVES)

74. *The Felix DeMoville house stood at the corner of Spring and Vine streets from 1857 to 1902. It was a brick structure with a wooden shingle roof and measured 56 by 42 feet. General Rousseau's headquarters was in it when the house was photographed in 1864.* (NATIONAL ARCHIVES)

[75]

[76]

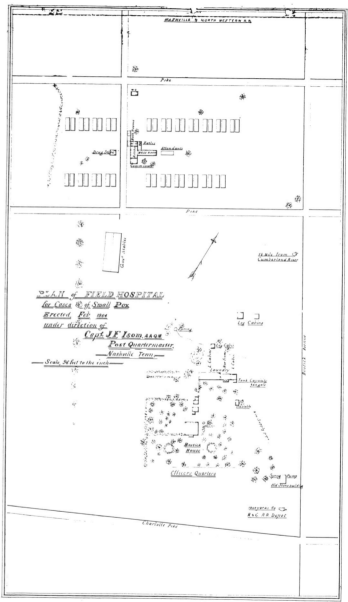

75–76. *H. P. Bostick was an attorney in Nashville prior to the war and had an office at 94 North Cherry Street. This brick structure on Charlotte Pike was his home. It measured 56 by 42 feet and had a wooden shingle roof. It is fortunate that the Federal army made a diagram of the layout of the grounds, a cross sectional drawing of the house, and a floor plan of it. The army even made plans for the tent field hospital for smallpox victims in the back yard, and of the tents themselves and the mess tents. The field hospital is seen in photograph 76.* (NATIONAL ARCHIVES)

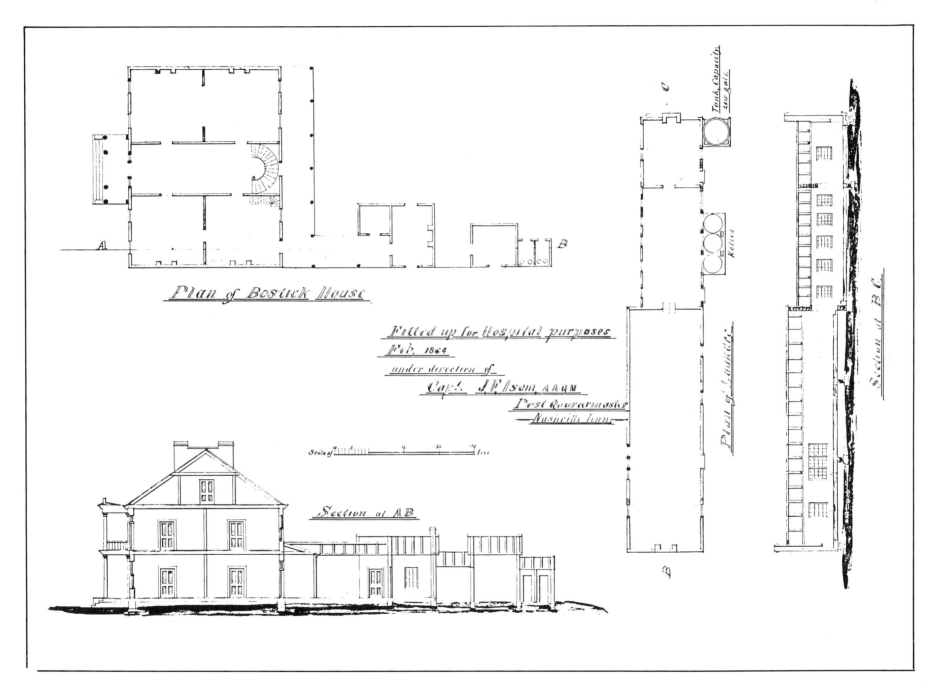

Plan of Bostick House

Filled up for Hospital purposes
Feb. 1864
under direction of
Capt. J. Ellson, A.A.Q.M.
Post Quartermaster
Nashville Tenn.

Scale of Feet

Section at AB

Plan of Laundry

Section at BC

Tank Capacity
400 gals.

Kettles

[77]

[78]

[79]

77. *A Federal soldier reverentially gazes up at the tomb of President James Knox Polk, in the side yard of Polk Place, near Union Alley and Vine Street. The tomb was designed by William Strickland.* (PHOTOGRAPH BY T. M. SCHLEIER FROM THE COLLECTION OF HERB PECK)

78. *This is a rare view of the James K. Polk home from the front. The side portico, facing Vine Street, and the garden and tomb of President Polk are at the right. Present day Polk Avenue is the driveway visible here from which T. M. Schleier photographed the home. From the revenue stamps on the back of this print, it appears to be a wartime view.*

This house originally had been built by Felix Grundy between 1818 and 1820 in the Federal style. James K. Polk read law there as a young man, and while he was president, he purchased the house for his retirement. In 1848 James M. Hughes was hired to redesign the house in the Greek Revival style. This had just been completed when a powder magazine exploded diagonally across Union Alley, leveling most of the house. Hughes then rebuilt it as seen here. (FROM THE COLLECTION OF HERB PECK)

79. *The tomb of President James K. Polk is shown as it originally was situated in the side yard of Polk Place at Vine and Union streets. Part of the service wing of Polk Place is visible in the background to the left.*

As a widow of a president, Mrs. Polk was respected by the Union army command and her residence and property were protected during the occupation of Nashville. The Tennessee Historical Society moved part of its collection to the sanctuary of the Polk home for safekeeping during the war. (LIBRARY OF CONGRESS)

DOWNTOWN NASHVILLE

Down the hill from the capitol, on the bluff above the Cumberland River, was the Public Square of Nashville. In April, 1856, a fire destroyed a number of properties there including the old Davidson County Courthouse, which is believed to have been designed by David Morrison. A new courthouse, designed by Francis Strickland and built in 1857, mirrored the capitol building, except that it did not have a central tower.

The square had several other new buildings. The Hicks and Ensley buildings, designed by Harvey Akeroyd, were both Italianate in style, as were the Morgan Company building and the Inn Block building on the north side of the square. On the east side was the publishing plant for the Methodist Episcopal Church South. The denomination had divided along regional lines, and the new southern body established its press in Nashville. A beautiful suspension bridge leading from the east side of the square tied Nashville to its sister city across the Cumberland, Edgefield. Sadly, the retreating Confederates burned the bridge in their panicky flight.

Running north and south from the square was Market Street, the main commercial thoroughfare of the city. Large buildings lined the street, while Broad, College, and Cherry streets also contained their share of Nashville's businesses. Many of these structures were seized during the war to be used as hospitals. Down the street, on the corner of Spring and Cherry streets, stood the as yet unfinished Maxwell House hotel, later made famous for the Nashville-blended coffee named for it.

These buildings were pressed into the service of the occupying forces, and their photographs are some of the most interesting ones we have of wartime Nashville. They help us to understand the sophisticated tastes of the community leaders in those days and to see what life in Nashville was like in the mid-nineteenth century. We see the unpaved streets, the rude sidewalks, the poor sanitation—and the lovely buildings. The contrasts were sharp. Because these wartime views heighten an awareness of the hard edges of life during that period, one can better understand the high death rates, the bleakness of poverty, and the luxury of wealth in those days through these images.

Nashville business depended on goods that were shipped to and from the town. The produce of area farms, the iron work produced at the T. M. Brennan foundry, the drugs sold at DeMoville's, and the building supplies offered at Stockell's were all carried by boat and rail. With the outbreak of war, most of these businesses suffered, since the river and rails were pressed into military use. Some businessmen, like Brennan and Stockell, had their property seized by the military. Brennan had been arrested and paroled for making arms to be used against the United States. Stockell had been indicted for conspiring against the lawful government of the United States. With the threat of treason and conspiracy trials—and the possibility of death sentences—hanging over them, many Nashville business leaders fled south during the Great Panic. Samuel Morgan and John Overton were two such men. However, Washington Barrow and William G. Harding were not as wise and were arrested for treason and imprisoned, with Harding permanently forfeiting his United States citizenship.

Nashville was fortunate, though. In falling without a fight, the physical infrastructure of the town was preserved. It was also spared being badly damaged because it was not attacked by the Confederates until December, 1864, and then they drew the Union forces out to meet them, saving most of the city from battle damage. When the war was over, Nashville was in a strong position to reassert its economic leadership in the region. Since the Federals had maintained the wharf and the rail lines, the city could quickly begin again to buy and sell goods. Compared to Richmond or Atlanta, where major battles had been waged—and lost—and where major damage had been inflicted by fire, Nashville was enviably situated to have a leading role in building a new South. In Nashville's case, it was a South with strong physical links to its past.

80. *The Public Square was the center of Nashville. This view of the northwest side includes College Street on the left and Market Street on the right. When the city was occupied, these buildings were seized by Federal authorities and used as ordnance stores.*

The Hicks Building, at the extreme left, was built about 1857 in the Italianate style from designs by Harvey M. Akeroyd. Two companies working out of it when the war began were Fite, Shepherd & Co. and William S. Eakin & Co. Both were dealers in dry goods and ready-made clothing. A grocer is next door. Beside it, at 47 Public Square, was Fall & Cunningham, dealers in guns, cutlery, and hardware. At 48 were A. G. Adams and Abbay & Gibson & Co., dealers in boots, shoes, and hats. At 49 was Morgan & Co., dealers in dry goods and manufacturers of clothing. The Morgan Building survived until July, 1974. The 1860 Haydon and

Booth map of Nashville shows the Morgan Building and a companion building to its right. The apparently fire-blackened cornice on the Morgan Building indicates that the missing structure probably burned between 1860 and 1864. One reason for the fire may have been the field forges parked in the street in front of the vacant lot and the Douglas Building. Douglas & Co., another dry goods and ready-made clothing merchant, was at No. 53 Public Square. Hugh Douglas, Byrd Douglas, Augustus W. Southworth, and George H. Thayer were partners in the company. The Criminal Justice Center now occupies all of this block.

The Rucker ambulance parked in the yard of the new (1857) courthouse is visible in a number of these views. It was the portable darkroom Barnard needed since it was necessary to develop the wet glass photographic plates soon after their exposure. (NATIONAL ARCHIVES)

81. *The view down North Market Street from the Public Square shows the back corner of the Douglas Building to the left and the Inn Block Building to the right. In the distance, to the right, is the bell tower on top of 82 N. Market Street, the site of the wareroom of Myers, Hunt & Company, carriage makers. The Union Hotel and a double Federal-style row house are at the left. This neighborhood was a mix of commercial and residential establishments. Boarding houses, such as Mrs. C. Lankford's, advertised that they "accommodated" day boarders, that "transient custom" was "solicited," and that all rates were "reasonable." Their location was described as "eligible." Nearby lived meat marketers such as James and T. B. Coleman, and such businesses as Alfred Adams's tinsmith shop, James Adams's saddlery, a bar, and a coffee shop.* (NATIONAL ARCHIVES)

82. *Myers, Hunt & Company, carriage makers, were in the buildings at 72 and 82 North Market Street. Both buildings are visible here. The carriages were made and repaired at No. 72 and sold in the carriage wareroom at No. 82. Two simple townhouses stood in between.*

The Nashville City and Business Directory For 1860–61 *listed the names and positions of the employees. C. F. Berry was the bookkeeper; G. M. Black, blacksmith apprentice; John Blake, carriage maker; George Boggs, body maker; F. Dunwell, trimmer; James Gillespie, blacksmith; D. Hancock, blacksmith; G. T. Hart, wheel maker; John T. Ingles, body maker; John Kennedy, finisher; E. Laurent, painter; John McKnight, painter; H. Osburn, blacksmith; J. Owens, painter; H. B. Quimby, blacksmith; A. Schenanberger, coach maker; Thomas Schusic, carriage maker; and W. H. Townsend, carriage maker. The Myers lived across the street at 81 N. Market Street. J. B. Lankford, a coach-smith, and James Lankford, a coach-trimmer, lived at Mrs. Lankford's boarding house at 90 N. Market St. W. S. Hunt, an owner of Myers, Hunt & Company, lived across the river in the affluent suburban town of Edgefield.* (NATIONAL ARCHIVES)

83. *The carriage wareroom of Myers, Hunt & Company is shown here. The building was 40 x 60 feet and was used as an ordnance store.* (NATIONAL ARCHIVES)

84. *Gate posts to a dismantled fence and gate, one piece of which is seen lying on the ground to the left of the post, are at the side of the courthouse. Market Street on the north side of the square is on the left and the river would be on the right. The three tallest buildings occupy the site of the old Nashville Inn, which, along with the old courthouse, burned on 13 April 1856. The volunteer fire companies were on strike and failed to respond to the great conflagration.*

Prior to the war, clothing merchants, druggists, a grocer, a liquor store, and a book bindery were among the businesses located here. The five largest structures measured 230 by 30 feet. During the occupation, three were used as medical storage facilities, and two were used as commissary stores. (NATIONAL ARCHIVES)

[85]

85. *The Southern Methodist Publishing House was on the east side of the Public Square between the square and the river bluff. The building measured 180 by 44 feet. The publishing house was established in 1854 after the Methodist Church split over the issue of slavery into northern and southern factions. Federal authorities used these facilities to print forms and myriad report blanks used by the army. The bridge would be to the right of the City Hotel, where Samuel M. Scott was the proprietor. The hotel is partially visible on the right.* (NATIONAL ARCHIVES)

86. *Also on the east side of the Public Square, this pair of Federal-style townhouses had adapted to the commercialization of the neighborhood by becoming the Jones Hotel. Twenty-five people came out to pose for Barnard, including one in the doorway playing a guitar. The plans show the layout of the hotel and its use as a part of Hospital No. 3. It measured 60 by 176 feet.* (NATIONAL ARCHIVES)

Side Elevation.

of old Hotel towards Wash Room.

88. *The Nashville City Hall and Market, believed to have been redesigned by Adolphus Heiman in 1855, was on the west side of the Public Square. Market Street divided it from the Davidson County Courthouse, which would be at the right, out of the photograph. A Conestoga wagon is in Market Street.* (T. M. SCHLEIER PHOTOGRAPH FROM THE COLLECTION OF HERB PECK)

87. *The 1857 Davidson County Courthouse, designed by Francis Strickland, son of the architect of the Tennessee State Capitol and the First Presbyterian Church, is reminiscent of the capitol. A third floor was added to the courthouse around 1910, and it was demolished in 1937. Notice the smashed windows. The Inn Block building is visible at the left and the Nashville City Hotel, where William Strickland last lived, on the right.* (TENNESSEE HISTORICAL SOCIETY)

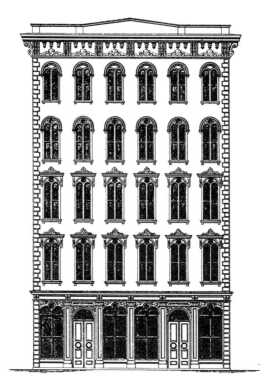

Front Elevation.

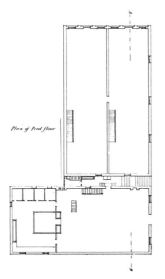

Plan of First floor

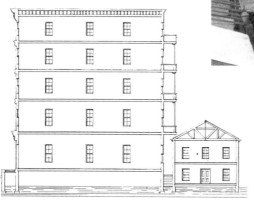

Section on line A B

89. *The Ensley Building, perhaps the most handsome commercial structure in town, was on the south side of the Public Square and measured 50 by 84 feet. Used in connection with Hospital No. 3 during the war, the building contained 200 hospital beds. A Sanitary Commission report complained of the many stairs to be climbed and of the poor ventilation. The facade elevation and the floor plan and cross sectional drawing are from the report.*

W. B. Grubbs's wholesale jewelry and fancy goods office was next door at 3 Public Square. Beside it, at 6 Public Square, was W. W. Berry & DeMoville wholesale druggists. (NATIONAL ARCHIVES)

[90A]

90. *The Watson House hotel was on Market Street south of the Public Square. Washington Manufacturing Company occupied the site in 1986. The Watson House was used in connection with Hospital No. 19 and measured 42 by 47 feet. The four-story building down the street on the left is the Morris and Stratton Building. The tall structure next to it behind the Rucker ambulance is the French & Co. Building. The first survives; the second was demolished in 1985, although it is shown in the modern photo at the right.*

The stone block post in the right foreground was a safety device for pedestrians, erected on a corner so that teamsters could not cut the corners too sharply and hit a pedestrian. (NATIONAL ARCHIVES, J.A.H.)

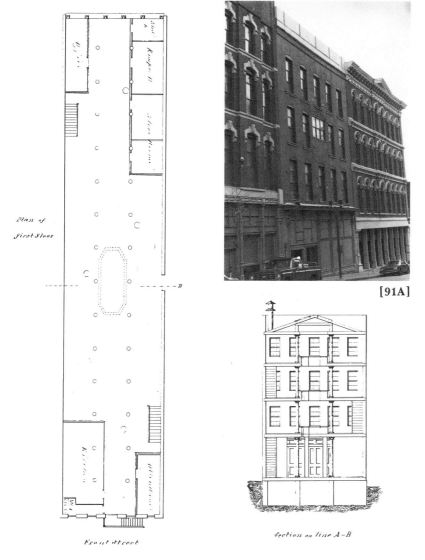

Plan of
First Floor

Section on line A - B

Front Street

HOSPITAL Nº 19

East Side of Market str. bet. Clark str. & Public Square

Owned by Morris & Stratton

Market Street

[91A]

91. *The Morris and Stratton wholesale grocers building was at 14 Market Street, near Clark Street. It measured 45 by 210 feet and contained 300 beds when the army used it as part of Hospital No. 19. The cross sectional drawing and floor plan show its interior. With them, it would be possible to restore the devastated facade. A skylight runs through the building.*
(NATIONAL ARCHIVES, J.A.H.)

92. *The Morris and Stratton Building is at the left, and the rear of the Watson House hotel is at the right, with the tower of the capitol visible over its roofline. These buildings were used in connection with Hospital No. 19.*

The filth in the yard may indicate why the mortality rates from disease and "doctoring" exceeded that of combat. This was medicine of a very primitive type. (NATIONAL ARCHIVES)

[93A]

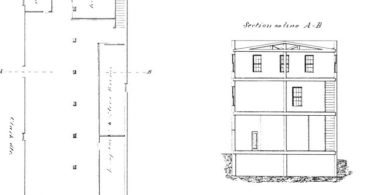

Plan of first floor

HOSPITAL N° 19
Brick-Building Corner of Market & Clark str
Owned by Franch

Section on line A-B

Market Street

93. *The French Building, at the corner of Clark and Market streets, survived until October, 1985, when it was damaged by arson and was demolished. The cross sectional drawing and floor plan show its inside configuration. It was a brick building with a composition roof and measured 46 by 108 feet. The Federal army used it in connection with Hospital No. 19.* (NATIONAL ARCHIVES, J.A.H.)

94. *This Market Street frame building, with a wooden shingle roof, measuring 42 by 80 feet, was used as Shop No. 3. It was presumably near College Hill since panoramic photographs taken from College Hill show frame buildings similar to this one.* (NATIONAL ARCHIVES)

[95]

[96]

95–96. *The building in the foreground on College Street was used as a government bakery during the occupation. It was made of brick, had a composition roof, and measured 55 by 188 feet.*

The building at the right with the bell tower and statue was the firehall and engine house of Broad Street Fire Company No. 2, located on South College near Broad Street. Captain William Stockell headed it prior to the war. The fireman statue is very similar to one from Kentucky in the collection of the Speed Museum of Art, pictured in photograph 96. See also photograph 53. (NATIONAL ARCHIVES, COLLECTION OF J. B. SPEED ART MUSEUM, LOUISVILLE, KY.)

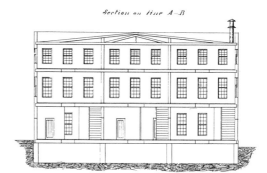

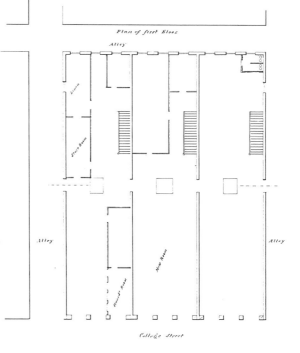

97. *This large commercial structure on College Street, between Broad and Spring, was used in connection with Hospital No. 16 as a 375-bed colored hospital. A large number of blacks are at the upstairs windows. The floor plan and cross sectional drawing show the interior layout of this 82-by-105-foot structure.*

Prior to the war, the building housed four commercial spaces. At number 13 was Groomes, Cavert & Co., a furniture store in which H. Griffith worked as a varnisher, C. Steinagle as a cabinet maker, and a Mr. Schell as a laborer. Number 15 contained Horn's Brass Band, a musical group, and the following painters: James F. Stevenson, W. M. Barnes, John Browder, William Cantrell, William Carpenter, David Little, L. D. Schull, W. Wilson, and John Wright. Robert Weitmiller's beer saloon was at number 17, and at 19 was Matthew Daly's beer saloon, Edward Hadra, bar keeper. (NATIONAL ARCHIVES)

[98]

[99]

98. *E. H. Ewing & Co., wholesale grocers, was in a brick building measuring 45 by 96 feet with a wooden shingle roof at 15 South College Street, at the corner of Spring Street. It was used as a carpenter's shop by the Federal troops.* (NATIONAL ARCHIVES)

99. *The Planter's Hotel was a brick building measuring 52 by 70 feet, with a wooden shingle roof. It stood at the corner of Deaderick and Summer Streets. Prior to the war, J. N. Alexander, the county coroner, was its proprietor. During the occupation, it served as Officers' Hospital No. 17.*

The tower to the left is on St. Mary's Catholic Church, designed by Adolphus Heiman and built between 1844 and 1847. Erected about 1850, Heiman's townhouse, which had identical detailing, was next door between the church and the hotel. Its projecting vestibule is visible here. (NATIONAL ARCHIVES)

PLANTERS HOTEL on Summer St.

100. *Three of Adolphus Heiman's buildings are visible in this photograph. To the extreme left is the corner of St. Mary's Church. Heiman's own home is next door, and down the street are the twin towers of the First Baptist* *Church. The old Planter's Hotel is in the center. This view looks south on Summer Street.* (T. M. SCHLEIER PHOTOGRAPH FROM THE COLLECTION OF HERB PECK)

101. *When Alexander Campbell took over the First Baptist Church of Nashville and formed the Church of Christ, the Baptists had to move to a new location. In 1837 they commissioned Adolphus Heiman to build a new structure for them on Summer Street, near Union. Dedicated in 1841, the church was made of brick, with a stucco facade and stone trim. It had a wooden shingle roof and measured 52 by 72 feet. During the occupation the building was used in connection with Hospital No. 15, and had a 150-bed capacity. It served as the First Baptist Church from 1839 (when the basement was occupied) to 1884, and as First Lutheran Church from 1884 to 1951. Commerce Union Bank now occupies the site.* (NATIONAL ARCHIVES)

102. *Christ Church Episcopal stood at the northeast corner of Spring and High streets. It was designed by Hugh Roland and built between 1829 and 1831.* (T. M. SCHLEIER PHOTOGRAPH FROM THE COLLECTION OF HERB PECK)

103. *The First Presbyterian Church had been situated on the corner of Spring and Summer streets since 1816. Two earlier buildings had burned down when, in 1849, William Strickland began construction of a new building which was dedicated on Easter Sunday in 1851. The cavetto cornice, the window and door surrounds, and the recessed panels along the roof line were all made of brick and painted to resemble stone. The manse stands behind it on Summer Street. James Stevenson's stoneyard is across the street. The church measures 60 by 108 feet, had a wooden shingle roof, and as part of Hospital No. 8 contained 206 beds. These floor plans are the first indication of the original interior configuration. Note that the tower roofs are pointed so that they could drain, not flat as they are today. Since 1955 when a part of the congregation moved to a new building on Franklin Road, this building has been known as the Downtown Presbyterian Church and is still in use.*

The two-story outhouse built by the Federal army was an attempt to solve the sanitary problem presented by a twenty-six-hole latrine in the side yard of the church. Although the latrine was closed in January of 1864, the solution was even worse. The two-story outhouse had four holes upstairs and four holes downstairs. The elbows to the drains were made of leather—and leaked. It did contain a stove for warmth, however. (NATIONAL ARCHIVES, J.A.H.)

[103A]

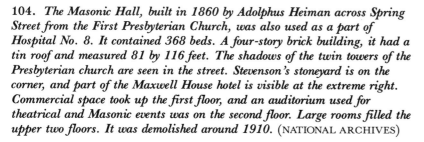

104. *The Masonic Hall, built in 1860 by Adolphus Heiman across Spring Street from the First Presbyterian Church, was also used as a part of Hospital No. 8. It contained 368 beds. A four-story brick building, it had a tin roof and measured 81 by 116 feet. The shadows of the twin towers of the Presbyterian church are seen in the street. Stevenson's stoneyard is on the corner, and part of the Maxwell House hotel is visible at the extreme right. Commercial space took up the first floor, and an auditorium used for theatrical and Masonic events was on the second floor. Large rooms filled the upper two floors. It was demolished around 1910.* (NATIONAL ARCHIVES)

105. *Situated on the corner of Cumberland Alley and Summer Street, the Cumberland Presbyterian Church was also used as part of Hospital No. 8. It was a brick building with a wooden shingle roof and contained forty-one beds. The sidewalks in Nashville apparently were left to the discretion of the individual property owners, for they vary greatly in these photographs.* (NATIONAL ARCHIVES)

106. *The Maxwell House hotel was begun in 1859 by John Overton, Jr., but the outbreak of war halted construction. At first the Confederates quartered troops in the incomplete structure and dubbed it "Zollicoffer Barracks," in honor of Confederate General Felix Zollicoffer. Later, the Federal army used it as a prison for captured Confederates. On 29 September 1863, a staircase collapsed as prisoners were being moved down it, killing four or five men and injuring seventy-five others.*

The building, which was made of brick, had a tin roof, and measured 175 by 160 feet, was finally completed in 1869. Minstrel shows, which were very popular in the nineteenth century, have filled the blank corner wall with their hand bills and posters. The Ravel Troupe, and Arlington, Leon, Kelly & Doniker's Minstrels are the predominant advertisers.

Cast iron acanthus leaves on the columns on the first floor, and terra cotta capitals on the pilasters above gave a classical elegance to the hotel's exterior. One cast iron acanthus leaf and one pilaster capital fragment, which were salvaged when the hotel burned down Christmas night, 1961, are in the collection of the Tennessee Historical Society. (NATIONAL ARCHIVES)

107. *This once elegant Federal townhouse, next to the Maxwell House hotel on North Cherry Street, has L. Rich's watchmaking and jewelry shop on one side of it and H. S. Peach's gas fitting shop in its basement. The brick building had a wooden shingle roof and measured 54 by 42 feet. Captain Jonathan F. Isom of the 25th Illinois used the house as his office in the Quartermaster Corps. It was there that he made his architectural drawings of occupied Nashville.* (NATIONAL ARCHIVES)

108. *The Bank of Tennessee, situated at the corner of Cherry and Union streets where First American National Bank's fountain is today, was used by the Federal army as its paymaster's department building. Erected in 1853, it was made of brick and stone, had a wooden shingle roof, and measured 50 by 88 feet. Francis Strickland was the architect and modeled it upon his father's Second Bank of the United States in Philadelphia.* (NATIONAL ARCHIVES, J.A.H.)

[108A]

109. *The Adelphi Theater was designed by Adolphus Heiman in 1850. At that time, it contained the second largest stage in America. It stood east of the capitol on the west side of Cherry Street, north of Cedar. During the latter days of segregation, it was a theater for blacks known as the Bijou. The capitol is seen at the right.* (T. M. SCHLEIER PHOTOGRAPH FROM THE COLLECTION OF HERB PECK)

[110]

[111]

110. *The Odd Fellows Grand Lodge was the home of the New Theatre in 1864 when this photograph was made. It stood at the northwest corner of Union Alley and Summer Street. Miss Emily Thorne, "the pet of the military," was performing there. The Shakespeare Saloon is on the alley side.* (T. M. SCHLEIER PHOTOGRAPH FROM THE COLLECTION OF HERB PECK)

111. *Hume School was Nashville's first public school building. Completed in 1855, it was torn down in 1910 to make way for the present building of Hume-Fogg Academic High School. The structure was on Spruce Street near Broad. Like the University of Nashville's Lindsley Hall, it was brick with a composition roof and was in the castellated Gothic style. It measured 160 by 180 feet. Federal authorities quartered railroad employees in it.* (NATIONAL ARCHIVES)

[112]

112. *The Shelby Medical College was chartered in 1857 by Dr. John Shelby and others, and opened on 1 November 1858 with eighty-five students. An indigent hospital was connected to it, which treated Nashville's poor and served as a teaching hospital. The school closed during the war and never reopened.*

The ground plot shows the location of the college at Broad and Vine streets, with a stable yard, refugee camp, and teamsters' quarters all located close by, and the photograph shows the facade of the college. Egyptian Revival pharaonic statues flank the main entrance. The tall structure at the right was the teaching hospital.

113. *The rear of the college is shown here. The teamsters' quarters are along Spruce Street and the teamsters are out "taking the air," as are their blankets.*

[114]

[115]

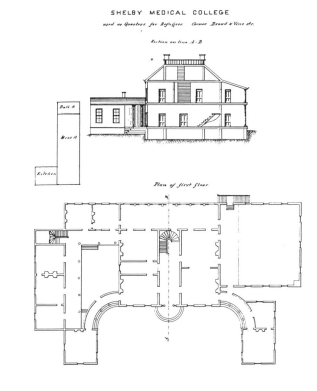

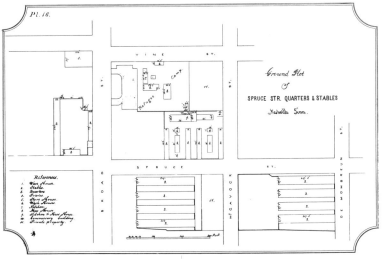

114–115. *Across Spruce Street (misidentified by Federal officials as Spencer) were the stable yards for depot transportation. Photograph 114 shows the tower on the Howard School, on the left. Photograph 115 pictures the second set of stables south of McGavock Street.* (NATIONAL ARCHIVES)

[116A]

116. *The handsome commercial building in the center and the right half of the double Federal-style commercial property on the right still survive on the south side of Broad today between Fourth and Fifth avenues. Both have been drastically altered, but with the aid of this photograph they could be restored. The squalid appearance of the buildings today stands in sharp contrast to their former grace.*

The main business housed in the four-segmented building at 77 Broad was William Stockell's shop. He dealt in plain and decorative plaster work, selling hydraulic cements, plaster of paris, plastering hair, fire bricks, fire clay, and terra cotta ware. The cross sectional drawing and floor plan show the interior of this structure. It was brick with a composition roof and measured 88 by 92 feet. Used in connection with Hospital No. 3, it had a 250-bed capacity.

The elegant Federal-style house on the extreme left, which is obscured by a tree, was also used in connection with Hospital No. 3. Its interior layout, shown in the drawing at the far right, closely resembles Hamilton Place in Maury County, Tennessee. (NATIONAL ARCHIVES, J.A.H.)

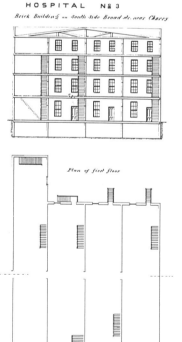

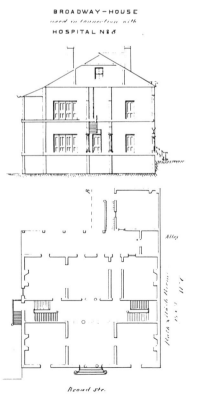

HOSPITAL Nº 3

Brick Buildings on South Side Broad St. near Cherry

BROADWAY-HOUSE

used in connection with

HOSPITAL Nº 3

Plan of first floor

Broad Str.

Broad Str.

117. *The corner of Broad and High Streets was the site of the stable for dray animals of the army hospital wagon trains.* (NATIONAL ARCHIVES)

118. *The Brennan Foundry was on the southeast corner of Broad and Front streets. Francis Strickland had the iron work on the tower of the capitol cast here. During the brief months of the war before Nashville's occupation, Brennan cast cannon tubes for the Confederacy. Two of these are on exhibit at the Tennessee State Museum.* (NATIONAL ARCHIVES)

119. *The label on this intriguing photograph states simply, "Nashville, Hospital laundry yard, July 1863." However, it would have been rare for white women to be laundresses at that time in this region. But with the coming of 70,000 troops to occupy Nashville, another occupation had grown rapidly—prostitution. Wartime estimates of the number of "women of pleasure" range from 40 to 1,500. The latter was probably more accurate.*

By July, 1863, venereal disease was rampant in the army, and so the military tried to control it by eliminating the chief source. The prostitutes were rounded up and shipped north by river. When Louisville and Cincinnati refused to accept the "cargo," the "ladies" were returned to Nashville. Still wanting to eliminate venereal disease and unable to get rid of
the prostitutes, the Federal authorities made them register, pay a license fee, submit to weekly health examinations, and stay clean. A special hospital to care for diseased prostitutes was established and supported by a tax placed on all the town's registered prostitutes. This system worked well, and the disease was controlled somewhat, although not eliminated.

If the date on this photograph is wrong, these buxom women may be America's first legalized and regulated prostitutes. The view appears to be on Market Street, and the women's VD hospital was on Market Street in the former residence of Catholic Bishop Miles, just north of Locust Street. (NATIONAL ARCHIVES)

[120]

[121]

120–121. *Hynes School was built in 1857 on the corner of Line and Summer streets. Federal authorities used it as Hospital No. 15 for the treatment of men who had venereal disease. It was made of brick, had a composition roof, measured 114 by 35 feet, and had a capacity of 140 beds.*

Photograph 120 shows at least sixty-seven men and one boy. Also visible is the photographer's Rucker ambulance, used as a mobile dark room, and a doctor's buggy. In photograph 121, William Strickland's Second Presbyterian Church is visible to the extreme left. It was demolished in 1979 to build the parking lot to the Criminal Justice Center. The floor plan and cross sectional drawing show the interior space of the school. (TENNESSEE STATE LIBRARY AND ARCHIVES, NATIONAL ARCHIVES)

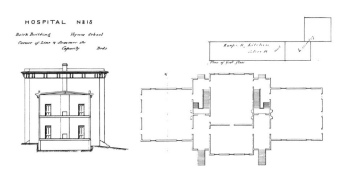

122. *The sulphur spring in Morgan Park, situated between College and Summer streets in north Nashville, was a link with the origins of the city. The mineral springs attracted large game animals. Ultimately James Robertson and John Donelson came to Middle Tennessee for the abundant game and the fertile land. Adolphus Heiman once owned this land, and Nashville industrialist Samuel Dold Morgan donated it to the city as a park.* (T. M. SCHLEIER PHOTOGRAPH FROM THE COLLECTION OF HERB PECK)

123. *Referred to by his men as "General Thomas's Circus Wagon," this mobile command post was quite a curiosity. Notice how the back wheels have been removed to make it easier to sit at the desk.* (LIBRARY OF CONGRESS)

[124]

[125]

124–125–126. *These views of Fort Negley show how the old grove of oak trees, which had been a popular ante-bellum picnic spot, had been cut off from the slopes of St. Cloud Hill, in order to make a free fire zone for the cannons in the fort.*

The first image is of the iron plated bomb proof gun emplacement. It was from Fort Negley that the opening salvo to the Battle of Nashville was fired on 15 December 1864. The second image shows the fort from the rail line below it. The eight covered cannon pits, the iron plated bomb proof gun emplacement and the palisade are all visible. The third image is of the inner defensive works.

After the war the fort fell into disrepair. Between 1936 and 1940 the W.P.A. completely reconstructed the fort. Due to its location in a deteriorating neighborhood, World War II, and the fact that it was an "enemy" fortification, the city of Nashville allowed it to fall into ruin. So it remains today. (LIBRARY OF CONGRESS, PHOTOGRAPHS 124 AND 125; NATIONAL ARCHIVES, PHOTOGRAPH 126)

[126]

[127]

[128]

[129]

127-128-129. *These photographs were taken during the Battle of Nashville. It is unknown who made them, but they all show the southern defensive line of the Federal troops. In photograph 127 Belmont mansion is visible in the haze of the horizon to the left. This view appears to have been made from near Fort Casino. In photograph 128 Fort Morton appears in the right distance, with the Franklin Pike crossing the valley diagonally. Photograph 129 is probably from Capitol Hill looking west.* (LIBRARY OF CONGRESS)

THE CITY AT MOCCASIN BEND

When the War Between the States started, Chattanooga, with a population of only 2,500, was more an idea than a place. But by the time the war was over, that had changed. The city had gained a national reputation as a transportation hub—"the Gateway to the South." The occupying Federal army had built a waterworks, a fire department, and a bridge across the Tennessee River, all of which Chattanooga lacked prior to the war. The Union occupation gave Chattanooga an industrial base upon which it could build in the years after the conflict.

The Chattanooga area was first visited by Europeans about 1540, when Hernando De Soto and his men walked through the region in search of gold and glory. They met the people of the Mississippian Culture, the mound builders, at a place called Chiaha, which is believed to have been either on Dallas Island or at Moccasin Bend near present-day downtown Chattanooga. The conquistadores spent nearly a month there, peacefully, with the Indians.

During the next three hundred years, the Mississippian Culture declined, the Cherokees moved in, and British explorers and their descendants visited and ultimately settled in the region. One Cherokee chief, John Ross, ran a warehouse, a store, and a river landing when the area was Indian territory and gave it his name: Ross's Landing. However, in 1838 coexistence with the Indians was forcibly terminated by these white settlers. In that year, on orders from the national government, most of the Cherokees were rounded up, placed in concentration camps, and force-marched to Oklahoma along the infamous "Trail of Tears." This cleared the way for the white settlers to elect their governing officials in 1840 and to incorporate in 1851. Thus was Chattanooga born.

Strangely, no mention is made in the accounts left by De Soto's men of the great natural beauty of the Chattanooga area. Since then, however, nearly everyone else who has visited there has been captivated by the beauty of Lookout Mountain, Walden's Ridge, Missionary Ridge, Signal Mountain, and Raccoon Mountain. The breathtaking view of Moccasin Bend from Lookout Mountain and the strange rock formations on the mountaintop itself have fascinated generations of visitors and inhabitants alike.

Among the artists who have painted the area were James Cameron, James Walker, James Hope, Alexander Helwig Wyant, Emma Bell Miles, William Posey Silva, Charles J. McLaughlin, and George Ayers Cress. George Barnard and J. B. Linn recorded the splendor of Chattanooga with their cameras before commercial development could mar its natural beauty. Countless tourists have posed for their own keepsake photographs from the Point Park area on Lookout Mountain, especially from Umbrella Rock.

James A. Whiteside, who came to Chattanooga when it was still known as Ross's Landing, was active in state politics and had several business interests in the settlement. After the Cherokee Removal, he helped attract the Western and Atlantic Railroad to Chattanooga and was one of the visionaries who foresaw Chattanooga's future as an industrial and distribution center for the southern Appalachians and beyond.

The Western and Atlantic line, connecting Georgia's capital city of Milledgeville with the settlement on the Tennessee River, was completed on 9 May 1850. At Milledgeville it linked Savannah and Charleston with the Mississippi drainage system via the Tennessee River at Chattanooga. To celebrate the South's link with the West by rail and water, a delegation came from Charleston and poured some water from the Atlantic Ocean into the Tennessee River. The salt and fresh water mixed, symbolically sealing the link between the Atlantic and the West.

Over the next ten years the settlement grew slowly. The Nashville and Chattanooga Railroad was completed in February, 1854, five years prior to Nashville's rail linkage to Louisville. On 28 March 1857 the Memphis and Charleston Railroad was completed, with the East Tennessee and Georgia (or Hiwassee) also opening about then. Thus, before the war began, Chattanooga was much more important militarily than Nashville because of its rail links north, south, east, and west. These advantages did not long evade the northern military commanders.

A devastating warehouse fire in 1858 prompted the settlement to establish a fire fighting organization. The fact that it was a warehouse fire that inspired this indicates the extreme importance of the transportation network and all of its kindred endeavors to the village. Storing goods, transshipping them, and marketing them were all important to Chattanooga very early, and nothing could be allowed to threaten this.

Harper's Magazine sent a reporter named Strother, or "Port Crayon," to visit this budding crossroads in 1858. His party stopped at the Crutchfield House, the local hotel which was a hive of activity, with speculators of all kinds present. He wrote:

> The hotel was swarming with people arriving and departing with the trains, east, west, north and south, hurrying to and fro with eager looks, as if lives, fortunes and sacred honor hung upon the events of the next hour. All the corners and byplaces were filled with groups in earnest conversation; some were handling bundles of papers, others examining maps. Rolls of banknotes were exhibited, and net purses with red gold gleaming through their silken meshes. In the confusion of tongues, the ear could catch the words: "plots," "stocks," "quarter sections," "depot," "dividends," "township," "railroads," "terminus," "ten thousands," "hundred thousands," "millions. . . ."

The Crutchfield House also felt the stirrings and rumblings of incipient war. When Lincoln was elected and southern congressmen were resigning their United States Congressional seats and returning home, one who stayed at the hotel when passing through Chattanooga was Jefferson Davis, soon to be the president of the Confederate States of America. Davis addressed a crowd of well-wishers and was reportedly denounced by William Crutchfield, the proprietor's brother, as a traitor. Thomas Crutchfield then removed his brother from the hotel.

By the spring of 1862, Chattanooga was occupied by Confederate forces and the Crutchfield House was converted into a Confederate hospital. In April of that year, soon after the capture of Nashville and the fighting at Shiloh, a panic gripped the citizens of the village. James J. Andrews had boldly led a party of Federal raiders south into Georgia where, at Big Shanty, they stole a locomotive and a few cars and set out for Chattanooga, attempting to destroy trestles along the way. The audacity of the exploit frightened southerners in general and Chattanooga's residents in particular, for they feared all manner of guerrilla raids and exploits. However Andrews and his men were captured, placed in Chattanooga's Market Street jail, and questioned at the Confederate post headquarters in the Crutchfield House. James Andrews would reveal no details about his raid or his local accomplices, and so he and seven other men were hanged as spies in Atlanta. Eight men escaped, and six others were exchanged as prisoners of war, receiving the first Congressional Medals of Honor for their valor.

Federal troops raiding in the Chattanooga area under General James S. Negley shelled the village in June, 1862. This caused still more fear and consternation among citizens, but the Confederates were back in force by July, under General Braxton Bragg. Interestingly, Bragg had been to the settlement almost a quarter of a century earlier when he participated in the Cherokee Removal of 1838.

On 1 August 1862, a southern institution was founded, the *Chattanooga Rebel*. Franc M. Paul was the publisher of this pro-Confederate newspaper, which was published in Chattanooga for about one year before it had to take refuge farther south. The *Rebel* was printed in the back offices over the Bank of Tennessee on Market Street and was a source of information for both northern and southern forces. Knowing this, the paper purposefully ran inaccurate information from time to time in order to mislead Federal authorities.

Conditions in Chattanooga became harsh when the village's meager services were overextended due to the influx of troops and refugees. Water became scarce by the fall of 1862 because only one well existed in the village. With the conversion of the Crutchfield House into a military hospital, another hotel was needed, and so in mid-November the Central House hotel opened on Market Street.

In December, 1862, Jefferson Davis visited Chattanooga en route to Murfreesboro to investigate the many complaints lodged against General Bragg by his staff, troops, and the press. Davis's personal friendship with such inept generals as Bragg and John Bell Hood would ultimately cost the Confederacy much. As a result of an interview with Bragg, Davis renewed his support and Bragg led the Army of Tennessee to defeat at Stone's River in Murfreesboro at the turn of the year.

By July, 1863, Bragg had retreated to Chattanooga. On 21 August, Federal Colonel John T. Wilder shelled the village from across the river and the next day the presses, type, other materials, and the families of the staff of the *Rebel* boarded a rail car for Dalton, Georgia. Many others left as well, including General Bragg and his troops—without a fight. Wilder's "lightning brigade" had panicked military and civilian authorities alike. With an old handpress and some type, a printer ran off a newsletter edition of the *Rebel* during this period, working in the downstairs bank room to be near the vault for refuge in case of renewed shelling. On 9 September 1863, the last Confederates left Chattanooga, and one hour later the Federals arrived.

The Reverend Thomas McCallie, the Presbyterian minister in Chattanooga, recorded in his diary that the village "never saw a more eventful day. . . . Not a child was harmed, not a woman insulted, not a man killed. . . . Here was a peaceful occupation of a city without any violence or outrage of any kind."

Once they had established themselves in Chattanooga, the Federal troops moved south to find the enemy and engage them. They did so at Chickamauga Creek from 18–20 September, but they were badly routed and fled back to Chattanooga. One of the few to distinguish himself in the Federal officer corps was General George Thomas, who held firm in the Kelly field and on Snodgrass Hill and then withdrew to Rossville, allowing the Federal forces to retreat safely. Now fear gripped the new defenders of Chattanooga, the Federals, as it had the former ones, the Confederates. Trapped within the settlement and surrounded by Bragg's now victorious forces, they awaited their fate.

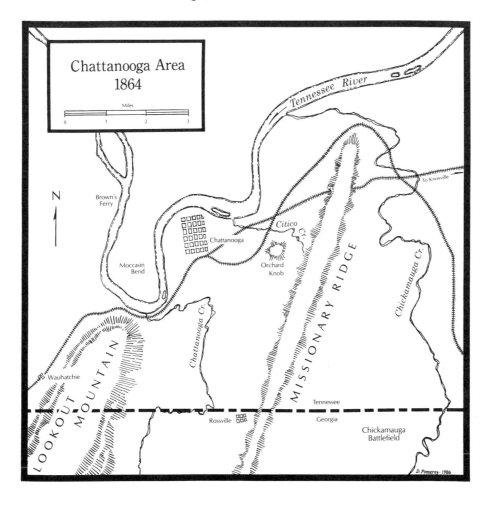

130. *The twenty-three-year-old village of Chattanooga is seen from the tip of Lookout Mountain. Most of the trees appear to have been cleared from the settlement area and the rail barn is visible left of center. General Sherman visited here in late March, 1864, and then moved his command to Chattanooga on 28 April. It was from Chattanooga that he launched his invasion of Georgia.* (NATIONAL ARCHIVES, J.A.H.)

[130A]

131. *The great natural beauty of the Tennessee River valley at Chattanooga captivated Barnard. From the point of Lookout Mountain he repeatedly photographed the rugged grandeur of the site of the "Battle Above the Clouds" during his brief stay in Chattanooga.* (NATIONAL ARCHIVES)

[132]

[133]

[134]

[135]

132, 133, 134, 135. *Even in time of war, visitors to Chattanooga's Umbrella Rock on Lookout Mountain enjoyed posing for a photograph with Moccasin Bend in the background, just as many generations of visitors have done. The natural beauty of the area and tourists' wishes for keepsakes remain the same.* (NATIONAL ARCHIVES)

136. *Moccasin Bend is on the other side of the Tennessee River in this view, with Chattanooga opposite it.* (NATIONAL ARCHIVES)

[138]

[139]

137. *Roper's Rock, on the west brow of Lookout Mountain near the point, was named for Jonathan Roper, a Federal soldier in a Pennsylvania infantry regiment who accidentally fell to his death from the rock after the "Battle Above the Clouds," 24 November 1863. Ladders are seen in the cleft at the left. The trees were broken in the battle.* (NATIONAL ARCHIVES)

[140]

138, 139. *Two views along the Tennessee River near Chattanooga. The Tennessee River follows the narrow pathways through the mountains that it has cut for itself over thousands of years. As the river rounded Lookout Mountain, it passed over a rocky outcropping in its bed. This produced a whirlpool known as "the Suck," which boats avoided by hugging the southern bank of the river. The T.V.A. has eliminated this navigational hazard.* (NATIONAL ARCHIVES)

140. *Barnard posed soldiers fishing from log rafts on the Tennessee River. Cameron Hill and Fort Sherman are to the left.* (NATIONAL ARCHIVES)

[141]

[142]

141, 142, 143. *The waterfalls and creek on top of Lookout Mountain seem to have fascinated Barnard. He photographed the rock-ribbed creek, the cascade, and Lula Falls and Lula Lake repeatedly. Most of these were* *probably made in April of 1864 when Sherman returned to Chattanooga.* (NATIONAL ARCHIVES)

144. *Battery Rock is seen on Lookout Mountain with a Signal Corps station on top. The line running diagonally through this print is the seam where the glass plate was joined together after being broken in two pieces.* (NATIONAL ARCHIVES)

145, 146. *These views of Lookout Mountain from the west show Lookout Creek and the rail line. In the move to break the Confederate siege of Chattanooga, General Hooker's forces moved down the creek, following the rail line to near Brown's Ferry. In the area along the creek, Confederate and Federal pickets were at some points only forty yards apart. They would sometimes meet to trade newspapers, tobacco, and coffee.* (NATIONAL ARCHIVES)

[146]

CHATTANOOGA BESIEGED

The Confederate siege of Chattanooga began when the Federal troops retreated there after their defeat at Chickamauga Creek in north Georgia. Trapped in little over one square mile of the village at Moccasin Bend, General William S. Rosecrans's Federal troops cowered at the foot of Lookout Mountain. To meet the expected Confederate assault, they razed houses on Chattanooga's outskirts and cleared the trees for a free fire zone, using the timber and lumber for blockhouses.

The Federal troops began to entrench and to fortify the area they controlled. W.F.G. Shanks recalled those days for *Harper's New Monthly Magazine* in January, 1868. "Residences were turned into blockhouses; black bastions sprang up in former vineyards; rifle pits were run through graveyards; and soon a line of works stretched from the river above to the river below the city, bending crescent-like around it, as if it were a huge bow of iron, and rendering it impregnable."

Shanks also wrote in the same issue of *Harper's* that "after the third week of the siege, the men were put on quarter rations, and only two or three articles were supplied in this meager quantity. . . . The hundreds of citizens who were confined in the town at the same time suffered even more than the men. They were forced to huddle together in the center of town as best they could, and many of the houses occupied by them during the siege surpassed in filth, point of numbers of occupants, and general destitution the worst tenement house in New York City."

From their siege lines atop Lookout Mountain, along Chattanooga Creek, along Missionary Ridge, and on top of Orchard Knob, Bragg's men grew increasingly restive. They wanted to follow up their victory at Chickamauga with a quick strike against their foes below. But Bragg was hesitant. Again, Jefferson Davis came to investigate the situation and again he sided with his old friend, and Bragg did nothing.

While the Confederates were wasting their advantage by not striking quickly, they were also leaving open the northern approach to the village over which Federal reinforcements poured in. The Federal authorities began to assemble an enlarged army to countermand the siege. Trains were rerouted from Washington to Indianapolis, Louisville, Nashville, and Bridgeport, Alabama. General Joseph Hooker was placed back in service and brought in 23,000 troops from Virginia. Sherman brought in more from Memphis, and General Thomas was placed in command at Chattanooga. But most significantly, General Ulysses S. Grant was given command of the entire western theater for the Federal forces. On 23 October 1863, he arrived in Chattanooga.

Grant immediately instituted an already-formulated plan of counterattack. He recalled in his memoirs that he rode out to inspect the lines, accompanied only by a bugler so as not to draw enemy attention to his presence. Along Chattanooga Creek he approached the Federal picket line. The Confederate pickets were in place on the opposite shore. The Federals called out, "Turn out the guard for the commanding general." As Grant was saying, "Never mind," the Confederate pickets also were heard to call out, "Turn out the guard to salute the commanding general, General Grant." He was thus honored by both sides at once.

On the night of 26 October, under cover of darkness, 1,800 Federal troops floated precariously and silently past the Confederate positions on Lookout Mountain and established a beachhead at Brown's Ferry downstream. On the twenty-seventh, this position was enlarged. The second phase of the Federal strategy took place the same day, when Hooker moved from Bridgeport into Lookout Valley. The only engagement to occur was a minor skirmish at Wauhatchie, in which the Federals were victorious.

The final phase in the relief of the siege of Chattanooga was a voyage by the steamboat *Chattanooga*, under the cover of night and in a driving rainstorm, to bring in 40,000 rations and 39,000 pounds of forage to the beleaguered defenders of the settlement. About midnight, on the twenty-ninth, the boat pushed its two barges up to Brown's Ferry, where the goods were unloaded and transshipped across Moccasin Bend to Chattanooga. This was necessary in order to avoid the Confederate guns on Lookout Mountain. By this three-pronged strategy, the siege was relieved.

Paradoxically, the inept Bragg chose the moment when the Federal forces had established a supply line and had been reinforced to move the part of his command under General James Longstreet upstream to Knoxville and attack the Federal forces there. This unexpected move disconcerted Washington. They assumed Bragg and Longstreet to be in a stronger position than they actually were in and asked Grant to relieve Burnside at Knoxville. Grant advised Halleck, the overall Federal commander in Washington, that he would relieve Burnside by driving Bragg into Georgia.

On 23 November 1863, Thomas moved across Lookout Valley and drove the Confederates back to the foot of Missionary Ridge. By doing this, he also took Orchard Knob. The next morning, Hooker, in fog and rain, dislodged about 2,000 Confederate troops who were lightly guarding the summit of Lookout Mountain. Now the stage was

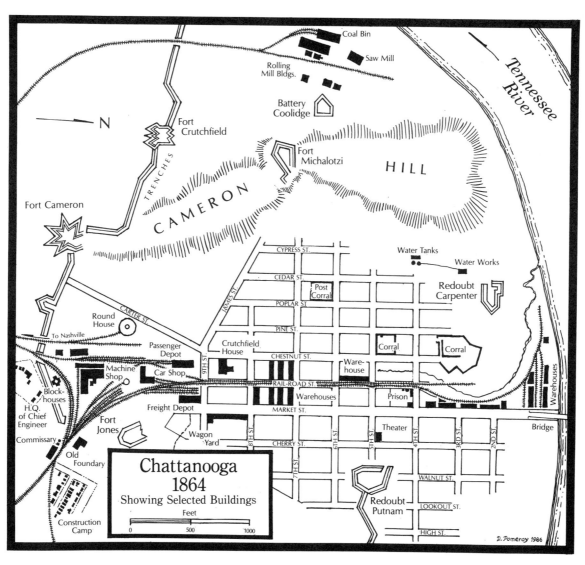

Chattanooga
1864
Showing Selected Buildings

Feet
0   500   1000

D. Pomeroy 1986

set for the grand climax. Sherman had marched his troops in plain view of the Confederates across the Brown's Ferry pontoon bridge and behind the hills to the north of the river. The Confederates thus thought that he had left Chattanooga to relieve Knoxville. In fact, he was moving his men across the river, concealing their movement from view by using the hills as a screen. On the morning of the twenty-fifth, Hooker came down from Lookout Mountain, crossed the valley, and took up the right flank nearest Rossville. Thomas commanded the center from Orchard Knob, and Sherman opposed the tip of Missionary Ridge from the left.

The two armies were drawn up against each other in one of the most beautiful natural amphitheaters in North America. The Confederates were on top of a narrow ridge, looking out across a broad valley toward the stone-palisaded top of Lookout Mountain and the broad arcing curve of the Tennessee River at Moccasin Bend. The Federals were on the plain below looking up at their enemy. Both sides, anticipating death and carnage, feared the coming struggle but were struck by the awful beauty of their positions. Then, an almost total eclipse of the moon took place. It was a scene worthy of Shakespeare. Sherman attacked, and the battle was on.

Hooker was slow to cross the valley, and Thomas—under orders—sat still until noon. Then he moved his men out from the center and also assaulted Missionary Ridge. A two-and-one-half-mile-long rank of troops was drawn up against the Confederates on the top. At this time Grant, from on top of Orchard Knob, gave the signal for a charge against the rifle pits at the base of the ridge. The men rallied and swept across the broad plain, overran the trenches, and, without orders, carried on to the summit. When Grant saw this, he was angered, possibly because he feared failure, and he threatened dire consequences for this unauthorized assault on the summit. When it succeeded, however, he no longer recalled questioning it.

An interesting aside on this charge is that young Arthur MacArthur, father of General Douglas MacArthur, led a column up the hill in the successful attack. For doing so he was awarded the Congressional Medal of Honor while only eighteen, something his son accomplished at a much later age.

By early evening on the twenty-fifth, the Confederate forces were retreating from the summit of Missionary Ridge, pulling back to the Dalton and Tunnel Hill area in Georgia. The next day, Thanksgiving Day, the dead were collected, guns were fired to mark the solemn Thanksgiving of victory, and Chattanoogans gathered outdoors to mark the day. The night before, Braxton Bragg had resigned his command, never to hold one again. Grant had further enhanced his military career and would soon become the commander of all Federal armies in the field.

No longer was Chattanooga on the front line of the conflict. The Federal army of occupation would settle in and Chattanoogans would learn what it was like to live under military control by the enemy, as Chattanooga was converted into a great forward staging area for the invasion of Georgia.

[147]

[148]

[149]

147, 148, 149, 150, 151, 152, 153. *The Federal troops guarding Chattanooga from Confederate attack were positioned throughout the Tennessee River valley. There were shore batteries, riverside camps, and camps in the valleys nearby. Photograph 147 shows a river battery with a Parrot gun. Photographs 148, 149, 150, and 151 show camps near Lookout Mountain, with the latter three along the river in the area that Interstate 24 follows today. The camp in photograph 149 is situated where the U. S. Pipe and Foundry Company is today. Photograph 152 shows a rather unorganized camp in a pass in Raccoon Mountain. A blockhouse, telegraph line, and camp are seen in photograph 153.* (NATIONAL ARCHIVES, ALL PHOTOGRAPHS EXCEPT 151; LIBRARY OF CONGRESS, PHOTOGRAPH 151)

[150]

[151]

[152]

[153]

[154]

[154A]

[155]

154, 155. *The Battle of Chickamauga took place near Lee & Gordon's mills on 19–20 September 1863. Union General Thomas L. Crittenden had been stationed three miles north of there when Braxton Bragg's Confederate forces overran it and forced the Federal troops back into Chattanooga. The Confederate troops then laid siege to the village.* (NATIONAL ARCHIVES, J.A.H.)

[156A]

156. *Orchard Knob (center) was overrun by Federal troops on the first day of the Battle of Chattanooga, 23 November 1863. Today, it contains numerous regimental monuments and is administered by the National Park Service. This photograph was taken from Missionary Ridge.* (NATIONAL ARCHIVES, J.A.H.)

[157]

[158]

157. *This view from the line of Federal trenches toward Missionary Ridge shows how many of the trees have been felled and how open the area was over which Federal troops had to charge to take the ridge line.* (NATIONAL ARCHIVES)

158. *The view of Lookout Mountain from Missionary Ridge, more than four miles away, is spectacular even today, but during the war most of its natural beauty was as yet unmarred.* (NATIONAL ARCHIVES. J.A.H.)

[158A]

Missionary Ridge.

[159]

[160]

[161]

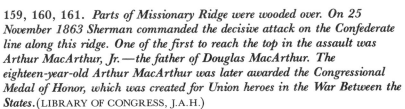

[161A]

159, 160, 161. *Parts of Missionary Ridge were wooded over. On 25 November 1863 Sherman commanded the decisive attack on the Confederate line along this ridge. One of the first to reach the top in the assault was Arthur MacArthur, Jr.—the father of Douglas MacArthur. The eighteen-year-old Arthur MacArthur was later awarded the Congressional Medal of Honor, which was created for Union heroes in the War Between the States.* (LIBRARY OF CONGRESS, J.A.H.)

162, 163, 164. *In March or April of 1864, Barnard made a three-part panoramic view of Chattanooga. He was standing in Fort Sherman from near Fifth and Walnut streets, looking toward Market Street when he took these pictures. At the left of photograph 162 are the passenger station and rail barn. The First Presbyterian Church, the brick structure with a wooden tower also to the left, was built in 1853 and occupied the corner of Market and Seventh streets until 1882. The Crutchfield House hotel, with its long line of chimneys, is beyond the church to the right. The brick building, St. Paul's Episcopal Church, is just to the right of center, with Academy Hill behind it. The settlement is relatively open here in contrast with the photographs on page 141.*

In photograph 163, the old city hall, with a two-stage bell tower above it, and the city market are at the left. The middle building of the three attractive brick structures at the center was a bank prior to the war. For a time it also housed the printing press for the Rebel, *a pro-Confederate newspaper. The architecture of the bank suggests Egyptian Revival. The white house with four columns across its front was Major Rathburn's house, at Sixth and Pine streets. Following his death at the Battle of Peachtree Creek, General James B. McPherson's body lay in state here, en route home to Ohio. Colonel James A. Whiteside's home, the two-story brick structure with two white columns, is at the right.*

Photograph 164 shows the Central House hotel to the left, at the corner of Fifth and Market streets. All of the buildings between the two-story brick store, which is three structures to the right of the Central House, and the end of the block were demolished by the Federal authorities. (See photograph 174 on page 143 for the same view after the demolition.) The three-story building with the bricked-up windows was erected at the corner of Fourth and Market streets by McCallie Brothers as a mercantile building. The sign over the door reads "Jail House" because both Confederate and Federal forces used it as a prison. Later used as the city hall, it was finally demolished in 1922. A military corral, seen behind the Central House, was situated in the area between Broad and Fifth streets. Another one, also visible to the right between Fourth and Second streets, extends back to Pine Street. Cameron Hill is to the left. (NATIONAL ARCHIVES)

[162]

[163]

[164]

[165]

[166]

[167]

165, 166, 167. *These are the faces of the Army of Occupation in Chattanooga. Their identities are unknown, but they were members of a court-martial group. It is not known whether they were defendants, witnesses, or members of the court.* (NATIONAL ARCHIVES)

168. *This view looks toward Cameron Hill and Redoubt Carpenter from the Government Wagon yard. First Presbyterian Church is to the right.* (NATIONAL ARCHIVES)

169. *Proud Federal troops show off the new firehouse, pumper, and ladder truck. First Presbyterian Church is at the left, on Market Street.* (NATIONAL ARCHIVES)

170. *Looking rather like a Russian Orthodox church, this blockhouse near Fort Jones guarded the Chattanooga rail yards. The troops in the foreground are standing in a formal garden. The headquarters for the chief engineer is to the left and the chimneys of the machine shop are in the background. The exact location is shown on the map on page 128.* (NATIONAL ARCHIVES)

171. *Lookout Mountain serves as a grand backdrop to Market Street. The Presbyterian church and the rail barn are to the left. Academy Hill, the Episcopal church, and the city market are in the center.* (NATIONAL ARCHIVES)

172. *The great number of very large warehouses erected by the Federal forces is readily apparent when this photograph is compared with photograph 171. The food, ammunitions, blankets, medical supplies, and other war materiel stored in these warehouses enabled Sherman to successfully invade Georgia.* (NATIONAL ARCHIVES)

173. *This view of Market Street was photographed from almost the same vantage point as photograph 163 and clearly shows how the Army of Occupation was creating a town out of the rude prewar settlement that was Chattanooga.* (NATIONAL ARCHIVES)

174. *During the occupation of Chattanooga, tremendous changes took place very quickly. Here the almost total destruction of the block of Market Street between Fourth and Fifth streets is shown. (Compare with photograph 164.) The rude huts, temporary shelters in which the troops lived, have been largely removed. The troops were now camped on Cameron Hill and at its base. When the Federal forces moved into Chattanooga, the settlement had no water works or fire department. Both were created by the army. In the cleared space along Market Street what appears to be two jets of water are visible. Perhaps this was a display of the new water line or of the pumper for the photographer.* (NATIONAL ARCHIVES)

175. *A new prison exercise yard was built on Market Street where the demolition had taken place between Fourth and Fifth streets. The built-up area along Market appears to have extended to Second Street. The clapboard house to the left has a sign in front which proclaims "Eating House."* (NATIONAL ARCHIVES)

176. *Having been incorporated only twenty-three years earlier in 1841, following the forced removal of the Cherokee and Chickamauga Indians, Chattanooga was still a raw settlement when Barnard photographed it in April, 1864. First Baptist Church is to the right and the rail barn is visible in the center through the trees. Beyond the church is Academy Hill. In the foreground is a Federal army trench.* (NATIONAL ARCHIVES)

177. *Photographed from present day Courthouse Hill near Fourth Street looking toward Market Street, this picture shows how relatively undeveloped Chattanooga was in 1864. There was only one primary street in the town. The water spout near the Central House hotel could be the pumper truck showing off for Barnard.* (NATIONAL ARCHIVES)

[178]

[179]

178. *George Barnard stood to the right of his camera with his hand upon it when he took this photograph from Fourth and Market streets, looking toward Cameron Hill. Barnard's shadow is in the foreground.* (NATIONAL ARCHIVES)

179. *Fourth Street is to the left. Across it, barely visible, is the jail. The long new board and batten building, on Market, was erected by the army as the issuing commissary.* (NATIONAL ARCHIVES)

180. *Situated between Fifth and Sixth streets, the two-story brick building and the board and batten structure were used by the army as the quartermaster's stores and warehouse.* (NATIONAL ARCHIVES)

181. *Fire buckets hanging along the roofline of the stable house of the Depot Corral and steps on the roof enable a bucket brigade to fight a fire on the roof. The Whiteside House is up hill to the right.* (NATIONAL ARCHIVES)

182. *The new prison and exercise yard was on Market Street between Fourth and Fifth streets. In the background are Cameron Hill, with a water tank on top, and the Whiteside House.* (NATIONAL ARCHIVES)

183. *The back of Major Rathburn's house at Sixth and Pine streets is to the right. Above its roof, the Central House hotel at Market and Fifth streets is visible. The jail at Fourth and Market streets is at the center. The long framed white structure is a barracks.* (NATIONAL ARCHIVES)

[184]

[185]

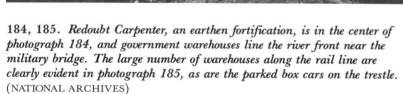

184, 185. *Redoubt Carpenter, an earthen fortification, is in the center of photograph 184, and government warehouses line the river front near the military bridge. The large number of warehouses along the rail line are clearly evident in photograph 185, as are the parked box cars on the trestle.* (NATIONAL ARCHIVES)

186. *A 200-pound battery was positioned on top of Cameron Hill, commanding a broad stretch of the Tennessee River. This was Battery Coolidge. The boy standing second from the right lived longer than any other Federal soldier, dying in 1956 at the age of 109.* (NATIONAL ARCHIVES)

[187]

[188]

187, 188. *This Lookout Mountain hotel was at the corner of Scenic Highway and Hermitage Avenue. General Hooker made his headquarters here in 1863, and Jefferson Davis stayed here after the war. George A. Ruble of Minnesota ran it as the Mountain Home summer hotel after the war. The battens have been painted a contrasting color to highlight them.* (NATIONAL ARCHIVES)

[189]

[190]

189, 190. *The Aldehoff School, on the brow of Lookout Mountain near Colonel Whiteside's hotel, appears to have been taken over by officers and a regimental band. When Fort Sumter was fired upon, the boys and girls enrolled in the school lit two barrels of coal tar and made secessionist speeches.* (NATIONAL ARCHIVES, LIBRARY OF CONGRESS)

[191]

[192]

191, 192. *Chattanooga's first waterworks was a gift from the United States Army. Situated at the base of Cameron Hill, the water works nears completion in photograph 191. A large military camp lies just beyond. The earthwork to the left is Redoubt Carpenter and the military bridge is behind* it. *To the center and right are military storehouses. The completed waterworks building is shown in photograph 192.* (LIBRARY OF CONGRESS, PHOTOGRAPH 190; NATIONAL ARCHIVES, PHOTOGRAPH 191)

HOMES IN EARLY CHATTANOOGA

In 1850 Oliver P. Temple visited Chattanooga. Years later he recalled that homes "were few . . . and they were insignificant." Yet there were exceptions. Civic leader James A. Whiteside had built a substantial Federal-style brick house as early as 1838 near the base of Cameron Hill. Dr. Philander D. Sims had also constructed a fine house for himself, as had Reese Bowen Brabson. Only Brabson's house survives, although in a greatly altered form, as it burned and was remodeled in the late nineteenth century. Today it serves as a restaurant on Brabson Hill near Fountain Square.

These three men were leading citizens of Chattanooga prior to the war and, along with the Crutchfields and other early promoters, they each helped to make the Chattanooga they envisioned a reality by encouraging business and industry.

James Whiteside was a banker, landowner, lawyer, and legislator. He had helped attract the first railroads to Chattanooga, built a hotel at the tip of Lookout Mountain in 1856, and had James Cameron paint a portrait of his family beside Umbrella Rock. In this inventive painting, James and Harriet Whiteside sit on an imaginary marble piazza overlooking Moccasin Bend and an infant Chattanooga. One slave tends their child while a second brings them drinks on a silver tray. Whiteside gave Cameron Hill to the artist for agreeing to live in Chattanooga.

Reese Brabson was a legislator and, from 1859 to 1861, a United States congressman. As a unionist, he remained in Congress until his term expired. He was also a gentleman farmer who raised livestock and tended his own orchards and vineyards.

Philander Sims was one of the community's earliest doctors and was among its first southern sympathizers. He served as a Democratic mayor after the war. His home was seized during the occupation, as were the homes of Whiteside and Brabson. Life under the gun could have its unexpected turns, even for unionist Brabson.

193. *This was a "loyal planter's home" on Lookout Mountain.* (NATIONAL ARCHIVES)

153

194. *General Sherman's headquarters proved to be too near the Tennessee River in the spring of 1864. The town was protected by a levee, but the levee overflowed.* (NATIONAL ARCHIVES)

195. *The Latner House at 110 First Street, another of General Sherman's headquarters, was drier. It is not known what happened to the roof.* (NATIONAL ARCHIVES)

196. *The house of Dr. Philander Davis Sims was on Market between Seventh and Eighth streets. His office, at the left, was used by the provost marshal, Linch Riversburg. This view of the house gives a misleading impression of the house's depth, for shutters enclosed a porch on the front of the house so that it appears as if the porch is part of the house itself.*

The shutters upstairs on the right are open. Dr. Sims had helped tend Confederate evacuees sent to Chattanooga from Nashville after its fall to the Federal army. In 1873 he was elected mayor of Chattanooga. (NATIONAL ARCHIVES)

198. *This unidentified house was used by the chief engineer, W. W. Wright, as his headquarters.* (NATIONAL ARCHIVES)

197. *Chattanooga's leading citizens, Colonel James A. Whiteside and his wife, Harriet, lived on the west side of Poplar Street, between Fourth and Fifth streets. Their house, built in 1838, was used by General Grant as his headquarters. Cameron Hill is visible to the right.* (NATIONAL ARCHIVES)

199. *Said to be the first frame house in Chattanooga with windows and door knobs, the Daniel Kaylor house was built in 1832 by Mat Rollins at Fourth and Cherry streets. Captain Brandon, the provost marshal, had his office in it, which may explain the line of troops waiting to get in.* (NATIONAL ARCHIVES)

200, 201. *During the occupation, the headquarters of the Army of the Cumberland was in this house between Brabson Hill and the Tennessee River on the second block of Houston Street. Barnard's shadow and that of his camera appear in photograph 201.* (NATIONAL ARCHIVES)

[202]

[203]

[204]

202, 203, 204. *The Kindrick house, on the left, served as General Thomas's headquarters in Chattanooga. In photograph 202, 52 captured Confederate guns from Missionary Ridge are displayed in a park. Twelve-pound Napoleons are in the foreground. In photograph 203 the Kindrick house is on the left and the headquarters for the First Topographical Engineers is in the foreground. These homes were on First Street. The third image, 204, again shows the Kindrick house and the park of captured cannons and caissons.* (NATIONAL ARCHIVES, PHOTOGRAPHS 202, 203; LIBRARY OF CONGRESS, PHOTOGRAPH 204)

205. *Headquarters to generals Rosecrans, Thomas, and Sherman, this house stood at the corner of Third and Walnut streets. Here, on 23 October 1863, Grant conferred with Thomas regarding resupplying Federal forces prior to their breakout from the Confederate siege of Chattanooga.* (NATIONAL ARCHIVES)

206. *Built in 1857 by Congressman Reese Brabson, this house served as General William Rosecrans's headquarters in Chattanooga. It burned in 1881 and was then greatly remodeled. Today it is a restaurant.* (NATIONAL ARCHIVES)

CHATTANOOGA AS A STAGING GROUND FOR INVASION

With the Confederate threat to East and Middle Tennessee removed after the South's defeat at Missionary Ridge, the Federal command reorganized. Both General George Thomas and General William Sherman were sent to Nashville: Thomas to garrison the town and Sherman to command the Department of the Mississippi. When Sherman reached Nashville in March, 1864, he thoroughly inspected his area of command and then in April moved his headquarters to Chattanooga to assemble an army of 100,000 men for his invasion of Georgia that spring.

Engineers and quartermasters swarmed over the town. They built a shipyard, a rolling mill, railroad car repair shops, machine shops, pattern shops, warehouses, barracks, corrals, stores, blacksmith shops, and wagon shops. All had to be ready by May, when the grass would be green and the army's horses and mules could forage off the land on their route south toward Atlanta and the sea.

The war had wrecked the Nashville and Chattanooga railroad between Bridgeport, Alabama, and Chattanooga. Bridges and trestles were down, tracks were torn up, and roadbeds were washed out. The U.S. Military Railroad took over the line and by February, 1864, had repaired it to a state that at least allowed stock to move along it.

By that time the railroads had become important to a swift ending of the conflict, the first in which railroads were used to prosecute a war. They were pressed into service to move men, weapons, food, horses, and medicine to the front. They were also used to move the wounded to hospitals in the rear. The Federals, with more miles of track and resources, used them more extensively than the Confederates.

The many buildings and operations the Federals built in Chattanooga to keep the railroads running were a tangible sign of the significance of railroads to the war effort. Some small scale industry had existed in Chattanooga prior to the war, but the Federals pushed Chattanooga into the industrial age.

When the war began, there were only two rolling mills in the entire South to reroll worn iron tracks: in Richmond and Atlanta. For their conquest of the South, the Federal army needed one in its area of control and Chattanooga was an ideal place. General Thomas testified before the House Committee Investigating the Affairs of Southern Railroads,

on 31 January 1867, that the time consumed in sending worn and guerrilla-damaged iron rails north to Louisville for repair badly affected the war effort and that the full-time capacity of the line from Louisville to Nashville to Chattanooga was needed to supply and maintain the armies in the field. In February, 1864, General Grant approved a plan to build an iron-rolling mill in Chattanooga. This mill was to become a significant economic factor in Chattanooga's industrial growth.

Confederate forces had begun constructing such a facility two miles from Chattanooga before they abandoned the village in late 1863, removing vital equipment as they retreated south. Finding the site too far removed from the settlement for easy defense, Federal authorities seized William Crutchfield's property near Cameron Hill for the location of their iron-rolling mill. Construction proved to be very expensive for its time, costing about $290,000. It was undertaken by the Construction Corps of the United States Military Railroad, which worked on it when not out in the field rebuilding damaged tracks. John and William Fritz designed and oversaw construction under the direction of General Daniel A. McAllum.

Three trains of rolls were in the rolling mill, whose sole purpose was the repair of existing rails, not the forging of new ones. Steam, supplied by a coal-fired boiler, produced the power to run the mill. For a twenty-four-hour double shift, it had a production capacity of about fifty tons of rerolled rails. The mill opened on 1 April 1865 and ran at half capacity until 5 October 1865.

Wishing to get out of the expensive business of maintaining railroads in the South, the government then sold the mill at public auction to John A. Spooner of Plymouth, Massachusetts. He purchased it for a low price of $175,000, but then had to pay Crutchfield for the land. The operation proved too costly for Spooner, and so he brought in Abram S. Hewitt, Peter Cooper, and others to form the Southwestern Iron Company, which had both northern and southern financial backing.

The Atlanta rolling mill had been destroyed during the war, but it reopened in 1866 as a competitor. When steel rails began to come into general use, though, the days of the Chattanooga mill were numbered. It closed in 1890, having dominated the area's economic development for twenty-five years.

207. *The Market Street Bridge over the Tennessee River was built by the military and survived until the great flood of 1867. It crossed about 100 yards south of the present span. The shipyard is at the right, across the river, at the foot of Cameron Hill. Barnard was standing about where Girls Preparatory School is now.* (NATIONAL ARCHIVES)

208, 209. *A military camp opposite Market Street Bridge is being dismantled in this pair of photographs.* (NATIONAL ARCHIVES)

210. *In 1864, Chattanooga was a small village, but its future as an industrial center was encouraged by the large number of iron-rolling mills, railroad shops, and foundries constructed there by the Federal army. At the time it was necessary for drivers to guide their teams around boulders in* *Market Street. The passenger station to the railroad is on the left with the river straight ahead. The Market House and jail (McCallie Brothers) are at the far end of the street. Across the street to the right is the Presbyterian church.* (NATIONAL ARCHIVES)

211. *An enormous pineapple sits on top of the belvedere of the Chattanooga railroad freight depot at Ninth and Market streets. The rail barn at the right was situated where the Bicentennial Library now stands.* (NATIONAL ARCHIVES)

212. *Another freight depot in the Chattanooga railyard is seen here.* (NATIONAL ARCHIVES)

213. *Built in 1858, the Chattanooga rail barn was a tangible symbol of the importance that railroads played in the growth of the town. Chattanooga's location at a natural passage through the southern Appalachian Mountains proved to be a great asset in its development as a transportation hub.* (NATIONAL ARCHIVES)

[214]

[215]

214, 215. *Confederate prisoners of war wait to be shipped to prisons in the North from the rail yards at Chattanooga. United States Secretary of War Edwin M. Stanton reported after the war that 26,436 southern soldiers had died in northern prisons, and 22,576 northern soldiers had died in southern prisons.* (LIBRARY OF CONGRESS, NATIONAL ARCHIVES)

216. *The Crutchfield House hotel, built in 1847, was one of the earliest permanent structures in Chattanooga. It burned in 1869 and the Read House hotel stands on its site today. Andrews' Raiders were confined in the Crutchfield House when they were captured. Part of Sutler's Row, where the troops bought personal items, is seen to the left.* (NATIONAL ARCHIVES)

217. *Cameron Hill is in the distance, the rail barn to the left, and the Crutchfield House hotel in the center. James Andrews and his captured companions must have walked past here as they were moved to the Crutchfield House for interrogation. The Adams Express Company office is also visible.* (LIBRARY OF CONGRESS)

218. *The War Between the States was the first major war during which troops and supplies were often moved by railroads. In Chattanooga plants were constructed by the military to repair the rolling stock and to maintain the rail lines. This gave Chattanooga an industrial base on which to build when the war ended. The foundry and machine shops are pictured here.* (NATIONAL ARCHIVES)

219. *The engineers who worked to win the war through moving men and supplies over the rail lines worked in these offices.* (NATIONAL ARCHIVES)

220. *The Chattanooga machine shops, which are here under construction, were used to repair the rolling stock on the Military Railroads.* (NATIONAL ARCHIVES)

[221]

[222]

221, 222. *The Chattanooga rolling mill, seen here both while under construction and later when in operation, was the only operating rolling mill in the South at the close of the war when the Federal authorities built it.* (NATIONAL ARCHIVES)

223. *The pattern shop for the United States Military Railroad was used to make wooden patterns for the wet sand metal casting, from which parts for locomotives and cars were made.* (NATIONAL ARCHIVES)

224. *The blacksmith shops, where the metal used in repairing locomotives and cars was beaten out, and the car depot, where railroad cars were stored, seem to have attracted attention as they were built.* (NATIONAL ARCHIVES)

225. *Repairs to locomotives, which were so important to maintaining the Federal forces in the field, were made in the locomotive and blacksmith shops.* (NATIONAL ARCHIVES)

226. *Metal replacement parts for the railroad were poured in the foundry and used in the car shop, both of which are seen here.* (NATIONAL ARCHIVES)

227. *The car repair shops are pictured while under construction.* (NATIONAL ARCHIVES)

228. *Railroad cars were overhauled in the car shops. The cars were damaged by guerrilla attacks and the heavy use by the military.* (NATIONAL ARCHIVES)

229. *Boxcars wait their turn in a line outside the car repair shop.* (NATIONAL ARCHIVES)

[230]

[231]

[232]

[233]

[234]

[235]

230, 231, 232, 233, 234, 235. *The hungry work crews on the United States Military Railroad were fed in these mess houses and slept in these barracks.* (NATIONAL ARCHIVES)

236. *The operation of the strategically important Chattanooga rail yard was run for the most part from this office. The foundry is also seen.* (NATIONAL ARCHIVES)

237. *A military store house from which the garrison and General Sherman's invasion forces were supplied.* (NATIONAL ARCHIVES)

238. *Commissary supplies for the railroad were drawn from this warehouse. It probably kept such items as lamps, coal oil, spikes, oil cans, and paper. Boxcar wheels lie in the foreground.* (NATIONAL ARCHIVES)

239. *Sleeping quarters for employees of the United States Military Railroad.* (NATIONAL ARCHIVES)

240. *The rail and telegraph lines around Lookout Mountain were a vital link in tying Chattanooga—and Sherman—to Washington and the rest of the North.* (NATIONAL ARCHIVES)

[241]

[242]

[243]

241, 242, 243, 244. *In order to care for horses and mules, the United States military authorities constructed large corrals in Chattanooga. The ones shown here were north of the rail line. Photographs 241, 242, and 243 show Academy Hill, the Confederates' Bragg Hospital complex, and the Masonic Girls' School. Photographs 242 and 243 picture the Quartermaster's Corral. The Officers' Hospital Corral is in photograph 241, with the corner of the Quartermaster's Corral to the lower right. Note the fire buckets on the roof and the roof ladder. A street level view of these structures and their design plans are found on page 182. The post corral is in photograph 244. A small Army Corps of Engineers castle sits on top of the building under construction. The whimsies used on some of these military structures were amazing.* (NATIONAL ARCHIVES)

245. *Water is kept on the roof of the government wagon shops in case of fire. Ladders lead up to the water barrels and additional fire ladders hang on the side of the shop. With the incredible amount of wooden construction* *undertaken by the United States military in Chattanooga, it is little wonder that they formed fire brigades and took precautions to prevent and fight fires.* (NATIONAL ARCHIVES)

246. *The floor plan and facade of the white two-story building at the right are shown in the accompanying drawing. The Hospital Department corrals are also seen here. The building with the central tower was the post shop. (See page 182.) Cameron Hill is in the distance.* (NATIONAL ARCHIVES)

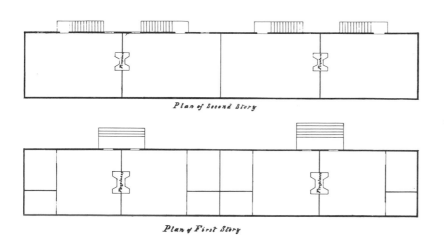

Plan of Second Story

Plan of First Story

Side Elevation

BARRACKS
One Building at
Engineer Corral, and one at
Engineer Shops
Chattanooga Tenn.

Scale 1:96

[247]

[248]

247, 248. *The Convalescent Corral was on the north side of the Tennessee River. The large rolling mill is seen across the river in photograph 247.*
(NATIONAL ARCHIVES)

[249]

[250]

249, 250, 251. *The horses and mules kept in the corrals near the foot of Cameron Hill, pictured in photographs 249 and 250, helped to break the siege of Chattanooga. The barracks for the Depot Corral are seen in* photograph 251. *A water tank halfway up the slope in both photographs 250 and 251 was part of the new waterworks built by the Federal army. The blacksmiths in photograph 251 appear to be largely blacks.*(NATIONAL ARCHIVES)

[251]

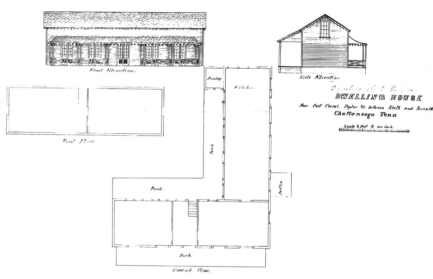

252. *The board and batten structure at the left was the office of the post quartermaster. The battens contrast nicely with the dark boards to give architectural highlight to the simple structure. The house at the center was used by the post quartermaster. Its plans and those of the post shop and corral to its right are in the drawing. The corral is on page 176. These buildings were on Poplar Street between Sixth and Seventh streets.*
(NATIONAL ARCHIVES)

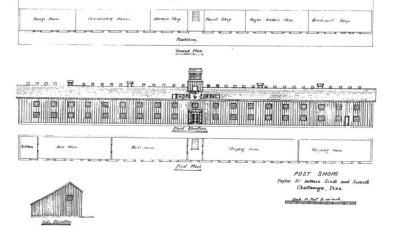

253. *Sutler's Row was on Chestnut Street between Seventh and Eighth streets. St. Paul's Episcopal Church is at the right. Most of the men seem to be outside the doors of the Etowah Restaurant and Saloon. Railroad Street was to the right.* (NATIONAL ARCHIVES)

254. *The office of the military railroad quartermaster was always a busy place. It was here that the clothing and subsistence for the army was accounted for. The reason for the bunting is unknown.* (NATIONAL ARCHIVES)

255. *The office of the chief quartermaster, who was responsible for provisioning the entire garrison, is under construction. Its plans are in the accompanying drawing.* (NATIONAL ARCHIVES)

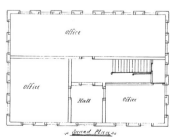
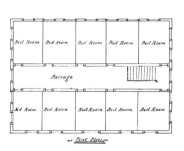

256. *Water barrels line the roof of the quartermaster's shops as a fire prevention measure. The many new wooden buildings and the threat of arson from the nearby Confederate troops must have made the Federal troops nervous. A grindstone sits beside the door.* (NATIONAL ARCHIVES)

257. *The towers of the Baptist and Presbyterian churches poke above the roof line of the quartermaster's warehouses.* (NATIONAL ARCHIVES)

258. *Equipment for the camps of permanently quartered troops was stored in these warehouses. Cameron Hill is at the left.* (NATIONAL ARCHIVES)

259. *The military engineers, who designed all of these buildings, railroad trestles, bridges, and fortifications, stored their supplies here.* (NATIONAL ARCHIVES)

260. *Clothing warehouses.* (NATIONAL ARCHIVES)

[261]

[262]

261, 262. *Weapons, ammunition, caissons, timbers, and tools were stored in this ordnance depot on Cherry Street near First.* (NATIONAL ARCHIVES)

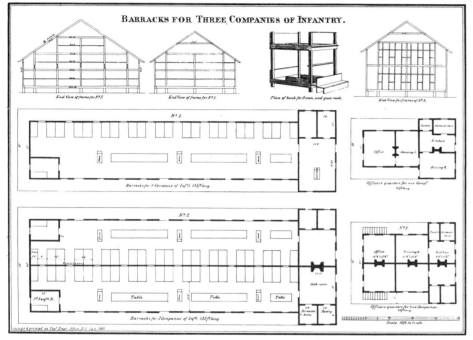

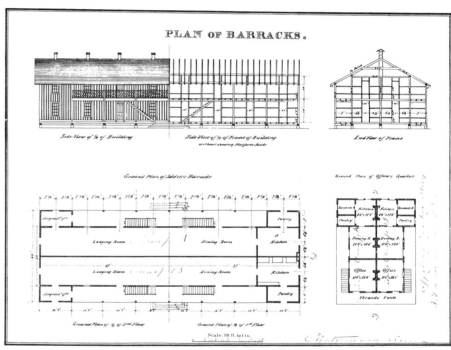

263. *Barracks for employees of the ordnance depot.* (NATIONAL ARCHIVES)

264. *Food for the military personnel and their mules and horses was stored in the forage depot.* (NATIONAL ARCHIVES)

265. *Prior to the war, the Masonic Academy stood on top of Academy Hill. It is visible to the extreme right. The wooden buildings were erected by the Confederates to serve as Bragg Hospital. Two ambulances are at the right.* (NATIONAL ARCHIVES)

SHIPS, SAWMILLS, A BRIDGE, AND BOREDOM

Once the siege lines had been lifted and the river and rail lines of supply reestablished, Chattanooga became first a staging area for a great invasion and then a boring backwater of war. During the two months that Barnard knew the settlement, first on his visit with Sherman in March, 1864, and later in April when Sherman relocated his command there, the shipyard and waterfront were busy areas. War goods were still being brought in to outfit the army then readying to march through Georgia. Sawmills were busy denuding the countryside of its beautiful trees to be converted into lumber for the construction of barracks, warehouses, commissaries, and hospitals. Barnard's views from Lookout Mountain show this devastation. The area below the mountain was stripped and mills were opened on the mountain to exploit its timber. Some of this lumber, and even raw tree trunks, were used to build the Tennessee River bridge. In the photographs the bridge appears to have been built of matchsticks, and yet it helped to keep the army supplied and in communication with the North.

The Citico Mound northeast of town, where a city water company intake plant is now situated, was used as a bizarre convalescents' garden during the late months of occupation. Arbors, garden benches, a pavilion, and fences all made this ancient burial mound into a refuge for the ailing troops. The mound was investigated by some of the troops and a report on their findings was filed with the Bureau of Ethnology. In the 1930s, the mound was again excavated—and removed.

When the war ended, immigrants were seen as bringing one solution to East Tennessee's postwar problems. The reconstruction state government advertised in the North and in Europe for people to take advantage of the economic opportunities in the area. Those who came were generally not exploiters of the freedmen, but rather of the natural and industrial resources at hand. Market Street was glowingly described in Chattanooga's *Daily Republican* of 9 March 1869 as offering "wealth to doctors and bankruptcy to life insurance companies."

However, the *Nashville Daily Press and Times* on 29 April 1867 lamented that there were "a large number of farmers in Tennessee who are pressed for money, and would gladly sell a part of their land; but no immigration comes to relieve them. Immigrants prefer lands of the strongly loyal portion of the state to the richest lands of this [Middle Tennessee] division, where there is a bitter opposition to the State Government. It is a remarkable fact that Missouri and East Tennessee are receiving more settlers than all the rest of the South. Immigrants want peace, and they naturally seek that in loyal communities." These new citizens, the same newspaper pointed out on 10 February 1867, "vote the Republican ticket as faithfully as they hew wood and draw water." This endeared them to their Republican neighbors in East Tennessee.

In 1867 Tennessee appointed the Reverend Hermann Bokum to promote immigration to the state. He placed advertisements in local newspapers and some read much like Sunbelt boosterism of today. Beginning on 8 December 1868, and running for nearly one month, Chattanooga's *Daily Republican* displayed this ad.

✱ ✱ ✱ ✱ ✱

WANTED IMMEDIATELY
ANY NUMBER OF CARPET-BAGGERS
TO COME TO CHATTANOOGA AND SETTLE

The people of Chattanooga, no longer wishing to stay in the background, and feeling the necessity of immediately developing the vast mineral resources surrounding them, by which they can place themselves on the high road to wealth, prosperity and power, extend a GENERAL INVITATION to all CARPET-BAGGERS to leave the bleak winds of the North and come to CHATTANOOGA.

It is unnecessary to repeat what is universally known, that our climate is mild and healthful; our soil fertile, and our mineral resources and railroad facilities unequalled in the world.

Those who wish to come can be assured that they will NOT BE REQUIRED TO RENOUNCE THEIR POLITICAL AND RELIGIOUS TENETS, as the jurisdiction of the Ku Klux and other vermin does not extend over these parts.

Persons wishing to immigrate will be furnished detailed information concerning any business, by addressing Box 123, Chattanooga, Tennessee.

VOX POPULI

P.S. Those having capital, brains, or muscle preferred.

✱ ✱ ✱ ✱ ✱

Due to the animosity of the "unreconstructed rebels" in Middle and West Tennessee, the statewide campaign brought worthwhile immigration only to East Tennessee. Even today, a large segment of Chattanooga's population is descended from the "carpet-baggers" who brought in the needed knowledge, ambition, drive, and capital to make over the little village of 2,500 into an industrial town of regional importance.

Chattanooga's fortifications were dismantled by the winter of 1865–66, and Tennessee, the last state to leave the Union, was the first to reenter it in the summer of 1866. John T. Wilder, who had shelled the town in 1863, became one of its leading citizens after the war and was elected mayor in 1871. The rolling mill, saw mills, and other war-born industries continued to serve Chattanooga in a new age. New people also served it, and together they made it into an important part of a reunited and growing country.

[266]

[267]

266, 267. *A boat on the Tennessee River is pulled toward the viewer by a tow line. Apparently Harry Fenn saw Barnard's work, for in* **Picturesque America** *one of his engravings shows a very similar scene.* (NATIONAL ARCHIVES, PHOTOGRAPH 266)

268. *Small packet boats, which were used to transport mail and cargo, could not get up enough power to steam through the whirlpool that formed where Suck Creek entered the Tennessee River. Therefore a line was tied to them and they were pulled (warped) through "the Suck." Here a steamboat going upstream, away from the group watching, is warped through "the Suck."* (NATIONAL ARCHIVES)

269. *A ship's hull takes shape on the slipway of the Chattanooga shipyard. Small packet boats seem to dominate the river.* (NATIONAL ARCHIVES)

270. *The river supply lines were as important as the rail lines in Chattanooga. The shipyard helped to maintain transportation lines up and down the Tennessee River. The large structure under construction here was a machine, boiler, and blacksmith shop. The purely decorative cupola would seem to indicate the Federal forces were confident they would be in Chattanooga for a long time since they were adding decorative touches to their buildings.* (NATIONAL ARCHIVES)

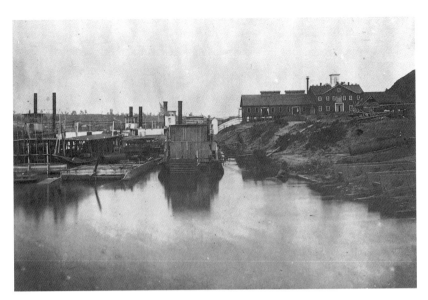

271. *The Chattanooga shipyard is completed, and at the left a ship is being repaired. A slipway is visible to the right.* (NATIONAL ARCHIVES)

272. *The commissary warehouse is to the right and the magazine to the left in this view near Market Street Bridge. For a view of the opposite side of the river, see page 162.* (NATIONAL ARCHIVES)

273. *Some of the troops housed in the shipyard barracks pose for Barnard near a ship's bell.* (NATIONAL ARCHIVES)

274. *This view of the shipyard shows how it was situated between Cameron Hill and the Tennessee River.* (NATIONAL ARCHIVES)

275. *Lookout Mountain at the left and Cameron Hill at the right frame this view of shipyard warehouses along the Tennessee River. Tied up in the foreground is the* Wauhatchie, *a steamboat named for a town downstream from Chattanooga where some of the fighting took place when the Confederate siege of Chattanooga was lifted.* (NATIONAL ARCHIVES)

276. *Market Street Bridge was being built by the Federals in March, 1864, when Barnard first saw Chattanooga. The plans in the accompanying drawing are for the construction of the bridge.* (NATIONAL ARCHIVES)

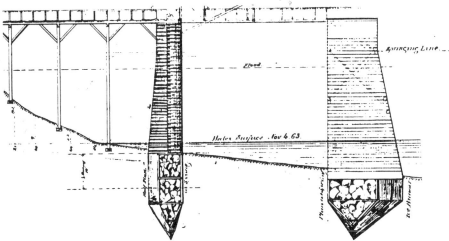

277. A water wagon is having its barrels refilled in front of the Market Street Bridge, which is undergoing construction. (NATIONAL ARCHIVES)

278. Blockhouses guard the draw span to the completed Market Street Bridge. Mules attached to a water wagon patiently wait for the teamsters to finish filling the wagon. (NATIONAL ARCHIVES)

279. *Part of the shipyard is visible downstream, at the left of Market Street Bridge.* (NATIONAL ARCHIVES)

280. *The draw span of the Market Street Bridge is to the right. A ferryboat, used prior to the completion of the bridge, is tied to the bank in the foreground.* (NATIONAL ARCHIVES)

[281]

[282]

281, 282. *The* Wauhatchie, *with a cannon on its foredeck, is tied at the foot of the Market Street Bridge. Other ships are berthed downstream from the bridge.* (NATIONAL ARCHIVES)

[283]

[284]

[285]

283, 284, 285. *The United States Military Railroad built its own hospitals in Chattanooga to care for its personnel. In photograph 283, railroad wheel* assemblies lie on the ground near the outhouses and engine cab roofs lie in front of a quilt being aired out. (NATIONAL ARCHIVES)

[286]

[287]

[288]

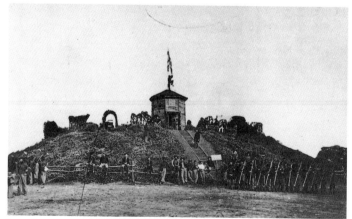

[289]

[290]

286, 287, 288, 289, 290. *The Citico Mound, an ancient Mississippian burial mound northeast of Chattanooga near the Tennessee River, was used by the Federal army as a convalescents' garden during the war. This series of photographs shows how it was landscaped in the spring of 1864 for that purpose. A two-story pavilion was built at the top, and vines, arbors, and bushes were added. Federal troops partially excavated the ancient burial mound and sent a report to the Smithsonian. The mound was removed about 1930 and the city waterworks is on the site today.* (NATIONAL ARCHIVES, PHOTOGRAPHS 286, 287, 288, and 289; LIBRARY OF CONGRESS, PHOTOGRAPH 290)

[291]

[292]

[293]

[294]

[295]

[296]

291, 292, 293, 294, 295, 296. *In order to build all of the structures the army needed in Chattanooga, it was first necessary to build a series of saw mills. Photographs 291, 292, and 293 are of saw mills along the Tennessee River. Photograph 294 was taken on the Glenview branch of Lula Lake Road near the head of the present Ochs Highway on Lookout Mountain. The two steam powered mills in photographs 295 and 296 were also on Lookout Mountain.* (NATIONAL ARCHIVES)

297. *Corrals on the Tennessee River near Chattanooga. Lookout Mountain is to the left.* (NATIONAL ARCHIVES)

298. *The commissary department and a hospital ward.* (NATIONAL ARCHIVES)

RAILROAD
TRESTLES

1 8 6 4

THE MAIN LINE OF SUPPLY

When the Federal troops captured Nashville in the spring of 1862, it was critically important for them to maintain both the railroads and the Cumberland River for the open and unimpeded transport of war goods, food stuffs, and troops. The Confederate raiders knew this, and so John Hunt Morgan and Nathan Bedford Forrest made raids against the rail lines that year. Morgan even succeeded in blowing up a rail tunnel in Sumner County that was a crucial link in the line to Louisville. With it knocked out of service, the Federals were forced to rely more upon the Cumberland River for their supplies and to finish the Northwestern Railroad.

The Northwestern line had been begun before the war and ran west of Nashville, past the Belle Meade farm and the Harpeth River, to Kingston Springs. The Federal army completed it all the way to the Tennessee River at Johnsonville where they built a large warehouse complex, which they used for the storage of goods pending their transshipment to Nashville or to one of the other fronts in the western theater.

Military and civilian railroad line repair crews were sent out to repair and maintain the Nashville and Chattanooga, the Louisville and Nashville, the Nashville and Decatur, and the Northwestern lines and their many trestles. As guerrilla harassments increased, some trestles even had guard posts erected and manned to prevent Confederate damage to them.

Knowing the strategic importance of these lines and how critical it was that they be maintained, Sherman made an inspection tour of rail lines as one of his first acts upon taking command of the Military Division of the Mississippi. Barnard accompanied him and took photographs of numerous rail trestles and of Knoxville. These pictures reveal much regarding the engineering of the day and how boring guard duty must have been at these isolated spots. In them we see wooden trestles, guard posts, huts that the troops lived in, and even dinner being cooked over a campfire. Some wooden trestles appear shaky and spindly looking, yet increasingly they were the main line of supply for the Federal forces.

Without the railroads it is doubtful that the South could have been brought back into the American nation, for they speeded the conquest. With rail lines in the North and the South, the government in Washington could reassert its control over the entire country once it controlled the railroads. Without these lines, the North may have had to end the war earlier—in a stalemate.

Most of the images reproduced here were only cursorily identified by Federal authorities. They could be Barnard's work, taken while Sherman was inspecting his new command in the spring of 1864. The brief identifications that are possible through research are given.

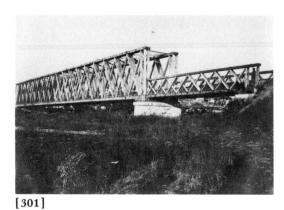

299. *The Big Harpeth Bridge in Williamson County.* (NATIONAL ARCHIVES)

300, 301, 302, 303. *The Rutherford Creek bridges Nos. 1, 2, 3, and 4 of the Tennessee and Alabama Railroad, north of Columbia.* (NATIONAL ARCHIVES)

[304]

[305]

[306]

[307]

[308]

304, 305, 306, 307, 308. *The Carter's Creek bridges Nos. 1, 2, 3, 4, and 5, of the Tennessee and Alabama Railroads, in Maury County.* (NATIONAL ARCHIVES)

309. *The Duck River Bridge of the Tennessee and Alabama Railroad, in Maury County.* (NATIONAL ARCHIVES)

310. *The Duck River Bridge of the Tennessee and Alabama Railroad, near Columbia. Dinner is cooking in the foreground.* (NATIONAL ARCHIVES)

[312]

311. *The Harris trestle of the Tennessee and Alabama Railroad, in Maury County north of Culleoka.* (NATIONAL ARCHIVES)

312, 313. *The Culleoka trestle of the Tennessee and Alabama Railroad looking west, in Maury County. Photograph 313 is the same trestle looking east.* (NATIONAL ARCHIVES)

[313]

[315]

[316]

[317]

314. *Interior of a bridge over the Tennessee River.* (NATIONAL ARCHIVES)

315, 316, 317. *Federal army engineers rebuilt this bridge after it had been destroyed by the Confederates. It was 780 feet long and 107 feet above Running Water Creek in Whiteside Valley, Marion County, near the Alabama-Georgia-Tennessee border. The Nashville and Chattanooga Railroad used the bridge. Photograph 317 was taken from the bridge, looking back down into the valley.* (NATIONAL ARCHIVES)

318. *A trestle bridge of the Nashville and Chattanooga Railroad over Chattanooga Creek.* (NATIONAL ARCHIVES)

319. *The Hiwassee Bridge of the Knoxville Railroad, near Calhoun.* (NATIONAL ARCHIVES)

320. *The Knoxville Railroad's Loudon Bridge, looking west.* (NATIONAL ARCHIVES)

321. *The Knoxville Railroad's Loudon Bridge, looking east.* (NATIONAL ARCHIVES)

[323]

322. *Barnard visited Knoxville with General Sherman's inspection tour late in March, 1864. Gay Street is seen at the center, across the Tennessee River. The Knox County Courthouse is the domed structure in the center, and the new jail is to the extreme left. The military bridge is to the right.* (LIBRARY OF CONGRESS)

323, 324. *The Strawberry Plains Bridge of the Knoxville Railroad, crossing the Holston River. Fortifications are visible in each photograph and a powder horn lies on the ground in the foreground of photograph 324.* (LIBRARY OF CONGRESS, NATIONAL ARCHIVES)

[324]

325. *The Bull Run Creek trestle and bridge of the Nashville and Northwestern Railroad in southwest Davidson County.* (NATIONAL ARCHIVES)

326. *The Big Harpeth No. 1 Bridge of the Nashville and Northwestern Railroad in southwest Davidson County. A guard house and a black man are at the right.* (NATIONAL ARCHIVES)

327. *The Big Harpeth No. 2 Bridge of the Nashville and Northwestern Railroad in southwest Davidson County. Buildings and a fire are visible on the opposite bank.* (NATIONAL ARCHIVES)

328. *The Big Harpeth No. 3 Bridge of the Nashville and Northwestern Railroad in southwest Davidson County.* (NATIONAL ARCHIVES)

329. *The Big Harpeth No. 4 Bridge of the Nashville and Northwestern Railroad in southwest Davidson County. A water tank lies across the Harpeth.* (NATIONAL ARCHIVES)

330. *The Big Harpeth No. 5 Bridge of the Nashville and Northwestern Railroad in Cheatham County. A log cabin and farm can be seen through the bridge piers.* (NATIONAL ARCHIVES)

331. *The Big Harpeth No. 6 Bridge of the Nashville and Northwestern Railroad in Cheatham County. A sentry stands at attention on the left.* (NATIONAL ARCHIVES)

332. *The Big Harpeth No. 7 Bridge of the Nashville and Northwestern Railroad in Cheatham County. A troop camp and a guard post are on the opposite banks. A hand car is on the bridge.* (NATIONAL ARCHIVES)

333. *Sullivan's Branch No. 1 trestle of the Nashville and Northwestern Railroad in Cheatham County, about ten miles west of Bellevue.* (NATIONAL ARCHIVES)

334. *Sullivan's Branch No. 2 trestle on the Nashville and Northwestern Railroad, in Cheatham County, 10 miles west of Bellevue.* (NATIONAL ARCHIVES)

335. *The rail trestle at Section 29 of the Nashville and Northwestern Railroad. This was either in Cheatham or Dickson County.* (NATIONAL ARCHIVES)

336. *Section 49's trestle of the Nashville and Northwestern Railroad. This also was either in Cheatham or Dickson County.* (NATIONAL ARCHIVES)

337. *Gillem Station trestle on Section 51 of the Nashville and Northwestern Railroad, in Dickson County.* (NATIONAL ARCHIVES)

338. *Hurricane Creek trestle of the Nashville and Northwestern Railroad, Section 54, in Humphreys County. Notice the telegraph line.* (NATIONAL ARCHIVES)

339. *Section 55 of the Nashville and Northwestern Railroad, in Humphreys County.* (NATIONAL ARCHIVES)

340. *Section 57 of the Nashville and Northwestern Railroad, in Humphreys County.* (NATIONAL ARCHIVES)

[341]

[343]

[342]

[344]

341, 342. *Trace Creek trestle of the Nashville and Northwestern Railroad, in Humphreys County.* (NATIONAL ARCHIVES)

343, 344. *Johnsonville, about seventy miles west of Nashville on the Tennessee River, was a supply center for the Federal forces in Middle and West Tennessee. A direct rail line connected it with Nashville. On 4 November 1864, Nathan Bedford Forrest shelled the warehouses, ships, wagons, and troops there, inflicting an estimated $2.2 million worth of damage. On 5 November, Forrest then withdrew to join Hood.* (NATIONAL ARCHIVES, LIBRARY OF CONGRESS)

345. *Men repairing the railroad track near Murfreesboro.*
(LIBRARY OF CONGRESS)

346. *The Hazen Brigade monument at Stone's River Battlefield in Murfreesboro is the oldest Civil War monument. It was erected shortly after the battle in December, 1862, and January, 1863. This is a wartime view of it.* (LIBRARY OF CONGRESS)

347. *Made in October, 1863, by an unknown photographer, this view of teamsters in a harvested corn field is in an area of the state not usually documented photographically this early. The caption on the photograph reads "Blue Springs, Tenn." Fighting took place here on 10 October 1863. This was part of a Federal troop movement near Greeneville.* (LIBRARY OF CONGRESS)

INDEX

Nashville and Chattanooga sections are indexed separately. The section on railroad trestles is indexed with Chattanooga. Numbers in italics refer to photographs. References to drawings are printed in boldface type.

NASHVILLE

Acklen, Joseph, 71
Acklen (family), 17
Akeroyd, Harvey M., 29, 67, 71, 81, 82
Architecture, 71-80
Asmus and Clark (architects), 31
Atlas to the War of the Rebellion, 59

Bank of Tennessee, 71, *102*
Barrow, Washington, 81
Bostick, H. P., home of, *78,* **78-79**
Brennan, T. M., 81
Bridges. *See* Railroads, bridges of
Buckner, Gen. Simon, 18
Buddeke, John H., home of, *30*
Buell, Gen. Don Carlos, 19; headquarters of, *76*
Buildings, Commercial: Capitol Boulevard, 76; Douglas, 82, *83;* Ensley, 53, *59,* 71, 81, *87,* **87;** French and Company, 88, *91,* **91;** Hicks, 71, 81, *82;* Inn Block, 81, *83, 86;* Market House, *53;* Morgan Company, 81, 82; 210 Broadway, *59*
Business locations: Abbay and Gibson and Company (boot, shoe, hat dealer), 82; Adams, A. G. (boot, shoe, hat dealer), 82; Adams, Alfred, tinsmith shop of, 83; Berry, W. W., and DeMoville (wholesale druggists), 87; Brennan, T. M.,

Foundry, *59,* 81, *107;* Daly, Matthew, beer saloon of, *94;* DeMoville (drug supplier), 81; Douglas and Company (dry goods and ready to wear merchants), 82; Eakin, William S., and Company (dry goods), 82; Ewing, E. H., and Company (wholesale grocers), *95;* Fall and Cunningham (hardware), 82; First American National Bank, fountain of, 102; Fite, Shepherd, and Company (dry goods), 82; Groomes, Cavert and Company (furniture store), *94;* Grubbs, W. B. (wholesale jewelry), 87; Horn's Brass Band, *94;* Morris and Stratton (wholesale groceries), 88, *89,* **89,** *90;* Myers, Hunt and Company, *83, 84;* Peach, H. S., gas fitting shop of, *101;* Rich, L., jewelry shop of, *101;* Shakespeare Saloon, *103;* Stevenson, James, stoneyard of, *99;* Stockell, William, shop of, 81 *106,* **106;** Washington Manufacturing Company, 88; Weitmiller, Robert, beer saloon of, *94*

Campbell, Alexander, 97
Campbell's Hill, 29

Cedar Knob, 29
Churches, Baptist: Cherry Street, *56-57, 65,* **65;** First, *32,* 71, *96, 97;* Primitive, *56-57, 64*
Churches, Catholic: Church of the Assumption, *30, 40;* St. Mary's, *31,* 71, *95, 96*
Churches, Episcopal: Christ, *52, 53, 97;* Holy Trinity, *53*
Churches, Lutheran: First, *97*
Churches, Methodist: Elm Street, *68;* McKendree, *32, 52, 53, 59,* 71
Churches, Presbyterian: Cumberland, *100;* Downtown, *99;* (*See also* First); First, *22, 32, 52, 53, 58, 59,* 71, *98-99,* **99;** Second, 71, *109;* Third, *63,* **63**
City Hall, *86*
City Hospital, 17, 71
City Market, *39, 86*
City Tannery, 27
City Wharf, *59*
Coal yard, 51
College Hill (area), 55-70
College Hill Armory, *56-57, 63,* **63**
Commerce Union Bank, 97
Craighead, the Rev. Thomas B., 55
Cumberland River, *31, 33, 43,* 55, *58*
Cunningham, George W., house of, *72, 76*

Davidson County Court-

house, *39, 53,* 71, 81, *84, 86*
Davis, Sam, 61
DeMoville, Felix, house of, *77*
Donelson, John, 110
Driver, Capt. William, 31

Eaton Depot, *53, 54,* **54**
Edgefield, 19, 81, 83

Fire Department, Broad Street Company, *59, 93*
Floyd, Gen. John, 18
Foote, Flag Officer Andrew, 18
Forrest, Gen. Nathan Bedford, 18, 41, 42
Fort Morton, *25, 112*
Fort Negley, *53, 56-57, 111*

Garfield, James A., *76*
Gattinger, Dr. Augustin, 55
Germantown, 30
Grant, Gen. Ulysses S., 18; headquarters of, *76*
Grundy, Felix, home of, *80*

Hardee, Gen. William, 18
Harding, William G., 81
Heiman, Adolphus, 55, 62, 71, 86, 95, 96, 97, 100, 102, 110; townhouse of, *95*
Hermitage Club, site of, *76*
Hospitals. *See* City Hospital; Tennessee State Hospital for the In-

sane; U. S. Army, hospitals of
Hotels: City, *85, 86;* Jones, *85,* **85;** Maxwell House, *32, 53, 59,* 81, *100, 101;* Nashville Inn, 84; Planter's, *95,* **95,** *96;* St. Cloud, *32;* Union, *83;* Watson House, *88, 90*
Houston, Robert, home of, *22*
Howard, Memican Hunt, 67
Hughes, James M., 80

Isom, Capt. Jonathan F., 50, 101

Johnson, Andrew, 32, 71
Johnson, Gen. Bushrod Rust, 55, 61

Kirby-Smith, Edmund, 61
Kirkpatrick (house), 22

Lafayette, Marquis de, 71
Latrobe, Benjamin Henry, 29
Lindsley, John Berrien, 55
Lindsley, Dr. Phillip, 55, 60
Louis Philippe, King of France, 71

Masonic Hall, *22, 32, 53, 59,* 71, *100*
Methodist Episcopal Church South, publishing house of, 81, *85*
Metropolitan Nashville/ Davidson County

Criminal Justice Center, 82, 109
Metropolitan Nashville Planning Commission, offices of, 55, *56-57*
Miles, Bishop, residence of, *108*
Miller, General, headquarters of, *74*
Morgan, Gen. John Hunt, 41, 42
Morgan, Samuel D., 29, 81, 110
Morgan Park, sulphur spring of, *110*
Morrison, David, 23, 71, 81

Nashville, 17-112; architecture of, 71-80; as Athens of South, 17-28; College Hill section of, 55-70; downtown section of, 81-112; map of, *73;* railroads in, 41-54; Tennessee State Capitol in, 29-40
Nashville City Hospital. *See* City Hospital

Odd Fellows, grand lodge of, *103*
Overton, John, 81
Overton, John, Jr., 101
Owen, Col. Richard, 55, 61

Peabody College. *See* Schools, George Peabody College for Teachers
Pearl, John; 18
Pearl, Louisa Brown, 18-19
Pillow, Gen. Gideon, 18

Plantations and estates: Belle Meade, 17, 72; Belmont, 17, 71, 72, 112; Hamilton Place (Maury County), 106; Hermitage, 74; Middleton Place (Charleston, S. C.), 55; Polk Place, *35,* 47, 49, *80;* Rose Hill, 55
Polk, James Knox, 35; tomb of, *80*
Polk, Sarah Childress, 80
Polk Center, *76*
Polk Place, *35, 47, 49, 80*
Priestly, Dr. James, 55
Public Square, 17, *20,* 81, *82, 84, 85, 86, 87, 88*

Railroads, 41-54; bridges of, *42, 43;* Louisville & Nashville, 41; Nashville & Decatur, 41; Nashville & Northwestern, 41; passenger depots of, *46,* (Nashville & Chattanooga line), *48;* repair shops of, *44;* trestle of, *30;* yards of, *46, 47,* (Nashville & Chattanooga line), *45, 48*
Roads and streets: Broad Street, 22, 26, 52, 55, *59,* 81, *104, 106, 107;* Castleman Street, *58;* Cedar Street, 23, 38; Charlotte Avenue, 38, *78;* Cherry Street, 52, *59, 65, 75,* 81, *101,* 102; Church Street, viaduct of, *47;* Clark Street, *89, 91;* College Street, *20,* 55, *59, 63,*

64, 66-67, 69, 74, 81, 82, 93, 94, 95, 110; Cumberland Alley, 100; Deaderick Street, 95; Elm Street, 56-57, 65, 68; Fifteenth Avenue, 23; Fifth Avenue, 106; Fourth Avenue, 106; Franklin Street, 55; Franklin Turnpike, 25, 112; Front Street, 59, 107; Gallatin Road, 55; Guthrie Street, 58; High Street, 33, 38, 40, 53, 76, 97, 107; Lafayette Street, 68; Lebanon Turnpike, 55; Line Street, 33, 109; Locust Street, 108; McGavock Street, 105; Market Street, 17, 55, 56-57, 59, 81, 82, 83, 84, 86, 88, 89, 91, 92, 108; Mulberry Street, 22, 63, 69; Murfreesboro Turnpike, 17, 28;

Nolensville Pike, 27; Polk Avenue, 80; Priestly Street, 55; Sixth Avenue, 38, 76; Spring Street, 22, 23, 26, 32, 45, 47, 48, 77, 81, 97, 99, 100; Spruce Street, 103, 104, 105; Summer Street, 33, 52, 56-57, 68, 95, 96, 97, 99, 100, 103, 109, 110; Union Alley, 103; Union Street, 80, 102; University Street, 55; Vine Street, 30, 35, 36, 40, 77, 80, 104; Water Street, 59; Williams Street, 22
Robertson, James, 110
Roland, Hugh, 97
Rosecrans, Gen. William S., headquarters of, 76
Rousseau, General, headquarters of, 77

St. Cloud Hill, 111
Schools: Davidson Acad-

emy, 55; George Peabody College for Teachers, 55; Howard School, 55, 56-57, 66, 67, 71, 105; Hume School, 71, 103; Hume-Fogg Academic High School, 103; Hynes High School, 33, 109, 109; Montgomery Bell Academy, 55; Nashville Female Academy, 17; Peabody Normal College, 55; St. Cecilia Academy, 17, 71, 72; Shelby Medical College, 17, 50, 104, 105; University of Nashville, 55, 56-57, 57, 71 (see also University of Nashville); Vanderbilt University, 55; Western Military Institute, 55, 61
Shelby, Dr. John, 104
Sherman, Gen. William

Tecumseh, headquarters of, 76
Slaves, 27, 34, 47
South Nashville, 55
Speed Museum of Art (Louisville, Kentucky), 93
Stevenson, stoneyard of, 100
Stockell, Capt. William, 93
Strickland, Francis, 29, 71, 81, 86, 102
Strickland, William, 29, 71, 99, 109

Taylor Depot, 52
Tennessee State Capitol, 17, 22, 29-40, 30-40, 45, 49, 53, 58, 59, 71, 102
Tennessee State Hospital for the Insane, 17, 71
Tennessee State Library, 71
Tennessee State Museum, 107

Tennessee State Penitentiary, 22, 23, 71
Tennessee State Supreme Court Building, site of, 35
Thomas, Gen. George, 32; command post of, 110; headquarters of, 76
Tilghman, Gen. Lloyd, 18
Theaters: Adelphi, 17, 102; Bijou, 102; New, 17, 103
Troost, Dr. Gerard, 55

United States Army: Assistant Commissary of Subsistence, office of, 75; Assistant Medical Director, office of, 75; Assistant Quartermaster, offices of, 75; bakery of, 93; barracks of, 26, 26; carpenter's shop, 95;

Chief Quartermaster, office of, 75; corral of, 28; forage house of, 50; hospitals of, 22, 22, 59, 60, 60, 61, 61, 62, 62, 63, 63, 64, 65, 69, 79, 85, 87, 87, 88, 89, 89, 90, 91, 91, 93, 94, 94, 95, 95, 97, 98-99, 99, 100, 106, 106, 109, 109; mess house of, 49; officers of, 21; post teamsters, building of, 58; printing shop of, 46; quartermaster office of, 101; railroad employees, quarters of, 74, 103; railroad repair shops of, 36, 37; shops of, 92; stables of, 49, 50, 105, 105, 107; supply depots of, 46, 51; troops of, 20
United States Franklin Shops, 24, 25, 25
University of Nashville, 55, 56-57, 57, 71;

Lindsley Hall of, 55, 56-57, 58, 62, 103; Literary Department Building of, 55, 56-57, 61, 62; Medical Department of, 17, 55, 56-57, 59; president and staff, housing for, 60, 60; steam plant of, 60, 62;

Walsh, Mother Frances, 72
Warehouses: Eaton Depot, 53, 54, 54; Taylor Depot, 52
Whelan, Bishop, 30
Wilson County Courthouse, 71
Women's VD Hospital, 108

Zollicoffer, Gen. Felix, 18; home of, 72, 76

CHATTANOOGA

Academy Hill, 136, 141, 144, 176, 190
Andrews, James J., 116, 167
Andrews' Raiders, 167
Army of the Confederacy, Bragg Hospital of, 190; prisoners of war of, 166
Atlantic Ocean, 115

Bank of Tennessee, 166
Battle Above the Clouds, site of, 119
Battle of Chattanooga, site of, 133
Battle of Chickamauga, site of, 132
Blue Springs, 221
Bokum, the Rev. Hermann, 192
Brabson, Reese Bowen, 153; home of, 160
Brabson Hill, 153
Bragg, Gen. Braxton, 116, 127, 128-129
Bragg Hospital (Confederate), 176

Brandon, Capt., headquarters of, 158
Bridges: Market Street, 162, 195, 197, 198, 199, 200; Military, 152; Tennessee River, 191, 213; See also Railroads, Bridges of
Brown's Ferry, 127, 129
Business locations: Adams Express Company, office of 167; Chattanooga Foundry and Machine Shop, 161; Etowah Restaurant and Saloon, 183; McCallie Brothers, mercantile building of, 115, 136-137; Southwestern Iron Company, 162; United States Pipe and Foundry Company, 130

Cameron, James, 115, 153
Cameron Hill, 123, 137,

139, 143, 145, 147, 153, 157, 161, 162, 167, 179, 186, 196
Chattanooga, 115-221; as staging ground for invasion, 161-190; battle and occupation of, 127-152; bridges of, 191-205 (See also Bridges); homes of, 153-160; maps of, 117, 128; panoramic view of, 136-137; riverfront of, 148 (See also Shipyards); view of, from Moccasin Bend, 121. (See also City Hall, City Jail, City Market, Shipyard, Waterworks)
Chattanooga Daily Republican, 191, 192
Chattanooga Rebel, 116, 117; building of, 137
Chattanooga (steamboat), 127
Cherokee Indians, 115, 144

Chiaha, 115
Churches, Baptist: First, 144, 185
Churches, Episcopal: St. Paul's, 136, 141, 183
Churches, Presbyterian: First, 136, 139, 140, 141, 163, 185
Citico Mound, 191, 202-203
City Hall, 137
City Jail, 116, 145, 147, 163
City Market, 137, 141
Cress, George Ayers, 115
Crittenden, Gen. Thomas L., 132
Crutchfield, Thomas, 116
Crutchfield, William, 116, 161, 162
Crutchfield (family), 153

Dallas Island, 115
Davis, Jefferson, 116, 127, 150
deSoto, Hernando, 115

Forrest, Gen. Nathan Bedford, 209
Fort Jones, blockhouse of, 140
Fort Sherman, 123, 136

Grant, Gen. Ulysses S., 127, 161; headquarters of, 157

Harper's New Monthly Magazine, 116, 127
Hood, Gen. John Bell, 116
Hooker, Gen. Joseph, 126, 127, 150
Hope, James, 115
Hospitals. See Army of the Confederacy, Bragg Hospital of; United States Army, hospitals of
Hotels: Central House, 116, 137, 144, 147; Crutchfield House, 116, 136, 167; Lookout Mountain, 150; Market House, 163;

Mountain Home, 150; Read House, 167; Whiteside House, 146, 147, 151

Jails: City, 116, 145, 147, 163; Military, 137
Johnsonville, 220

Kaylor, Daniel, home of, 158
Kindrick house, 159
Knox County Courthouse, 215
Knox County Jail, 215

Latner house, 155
Lee and Gordon, mills of, 132
Longstreet, Gen. James, 127
Lookout Mountain, 115, 118, 119, 127, 128, 134, 141, 151, 196; Battery Rock of, 126; camps on, 130-131; devastation of, 191;

home on, 153; Point Park area of, 115; rail lines on, 175; Roper's Rock on, 122; Umbrella Rock of, 115, 120; waterfalls on, 124
Lookout Valley, 128
Lula Falls, 124
Lula Lake, 124

McCallum, Gen. Daniel A., 161
MacArthur, Arthur, 128-129, 135
MacArthur, Gen. Douglas, 128-129
McCallie, the Rev. Thomas, 117
McLaughlin, Charles J., 115
McPherson, Gen. James B., 136-137
Miles, Emma Bell, 115
Missionary Ridge, 115, 127, 128-129, 134, 135
Moccasin Bend, 115, 120, 121, 128

Morgan, Gen. John Hunt, 209

Nashville Daily Press and Times, 191
Nashville, 116, 161
Negley, Gen. James S., 116

Orchard Knob, 127, 128-129, *133*

Paul, Franc M., 116
Picturesque America, 193
"Port Crayon," 116

Raccoon Mountain, 115; camp on, *131*
Railroads, 161-162, 209-221; blacksmith shops of, *169;* employee dormitories of, *175;* engineers, offices of, *168;* foundry and machine shops of, *168, 170;* freight depot of, *164;* iron-rolling mills for, 161, 162, *169, 180;* locomotive shops of, *170;* machine shops of, *168;* mess houses of, *172-173;* offices of, *174;* passenger stations for, *136, 163;* pattern shop of, *169;* rail barns

of, *144, 164, 165, 167;* railyards, *166;* repair shops of, *171;* tracks of, *221;* warehouse of, *174*
Railroads, Bridges of: Big Harpeth (Cheatham County), *217;* Big Harpeth (Davidson County), *216;* Big Harpeth (Williamson County), *210;* Bull Run Creek (Davidson County), *215;* Carter's Creek (Maury County), *211;* Chattanooga Creek, *214;* Duck River, *212;* Hiwassee, *214;* Loudon, *214;* Running Water Creek (Marion County), *213;* Rutherford Creek, *210;* Strawberry Plains, *215.* See also Bridges.
Railroads (lines): Knoxville, *214;* Louisville and Nashville, 209; Memphis and Charleston, 115; Nashville and Chattanooga, 115, 209, 213-214; Nashville and Decatur, 209; Nashville and Northwestern, 215-220,

(Humphreys County) 219; Northwestern, 209; Tennessee and Alabama, 210-212; Western and Atlantic, 115
Railroads, Trestles of, 218-219; Culleoka (Maury County), *212;* Gillem Station (Dickson County), *219;* Harris (Maury County), *212;* Hurricane Creek (Humphreys County), *219;* Sullivan's Branch (Cheatham County), *218;* Trace Creek (Humphreys County), *220*
Rathburn, Major, home of, *137, 147*
Rivers, streams, and creeks: Chattanooga Creek, 127; Chickamauga Creek, 117; Holston River, *215;* Lookout Creek, *126;* Tennessee River, 115, *123, 162, 196;* bank of, *195;* battery on, *130-131;* boats on, *193, 194;* corrals along, *206;* fishing in, *123;* warehouses along, *196.*

See also Railroads, Bridges of; Railroads, Trestles of.
Riversburg, Linch, office of, *156*
Roads and streets: Broad Street, 136-137; Cherry Street, 158, 187; Fifth Street, 136-137, 143, 146, 147, 157; First Street, 159, 187; Fourth Street, 136-137, 143, 144, *145,* 147, 157, 158; Gay Street (Knoxville), *215;* Hermitage Avenue, 150; Houston Street, 158; Lula Lake Road, *205;* Market Street, 116, *136-137, 141, 142, 143, 144, 145,* 147, *163,* 164, 191; Ninth Street, 164; Ochs Highway, 205; Pine Street, 136-137, *147;* Poplar Street, 157, 182; Railroad Street, 183; Scenic Highway, 150; Second Street, 136-137, 143; Seventh Street, 136, 182; Sixth Street, 136-137, 146, 147; South Street, 182; Third Street, 160; Walnut

Street, 136-137, 160
Rosecrans, Gen. William S., 127; headquarters of, *160*
Ross, John, 115
Ross's Landing, 115

Schools: Aldehoff School, *151;* Girls Preparatory School, 162; Masonic Academy, 190; Masonic Girls School, *176*
Shanks, W. F. G., 127
Sherman, Gen. William Tecumseh, 118, 127, 128, 161, 209; headquarters of, *154*
Shipyard, 162, 194, 195, *196,* 199
Signal Mountain, 115
Silva, William Posey, 115
Sims, Dr. Philander D., 153; home of, *156*
Snodgrass Hill, 117
Spooner, John A., 162
Stanton, Edwin M., 166
Stone's River Battlefield, Hazen Brigade monument of, *221*
Strother (reporter), 116
"The Suck," 123, *194*
Suttler's Row, 167, *183*

Temple, Oliver P., 153

Thomas, Gen. George, 117, 127, 128, 161

United States Army: Army of the Cumberland, headquarters of, *158;* barracks of, 147, **179**, 181, **188**, *189;* Battery Coolidge of, *149;* camps of, *152, 162;* Chief Railroad Engineer, headquarters of, *140;* clothing warehouse of, *186;* convalescent garden for, *202-203;* corrals of, *136-137, 146, 176-177, 179, 180, 181, 182, 206;* firehouse of, *140;* forage depot of, *190;* generals, headquarters of, *160;* hospitals of, *201, 206;* issuing commissary of, *145;* ordnance depot of, *187;* prison and exercise yards of, *143, 147;* quartermaster offices of, *182, 183-184,* **184**; quartermaster's shops of, *185;* quartermaster's stores of, *146;* quartermaster's warehouses of, *185;* Redoubt Carpen-

ter, fortifications of, *148, 152;* sawmills for, *205;* shipyard barracks of, *195;* Signal Corps station of, *126;* storehouses of, *152, 174, 186;* trench of, *144;* troops of, *138;* wagon shops of, *178;* warehouses of, 141, 186

Walden's Ridge, 115
Walker, James, 115
Warehouses, *148. See also* United States Army, warehouses of.
Water works, *152, 181,* 202-203
Wauhatchie (steamboat), 196, *200*
Wauhatchie, 127
Whiteside, Harriet, 153; home of, *136-137, 157*
Whiteside, Col. James A., 115, 153; home of, *136-137, 157*
Wilder, Gen. John T., 116, 192
Wright, W. W., headquarters of, *157*
Wyant, Alexander Helwig, 115